HOW INVESTING IN COMMERCIAL PROPERTY REALLY WORKS

MARTIN ROTH + CHRIS LANG

Wrightbooks

First published 2003 by Wrightbooks
an imprint of John Wiley & Sons Australia, Ltd
33 Park Road, Milton, Qld 4064

Offices also in Sydney and Melbourne

Typeset in 12/14.4 pt AGaramond

© Martin Roth and Chris Lang 2003

National Library of Australia Cataloguing-in-Publication data:

Roth, Martin.

How investing in commercial property really works.

Includes index.

ISBN 0 7016 3808 7.

1. Commercial real estate. 2. Investments. I. Lang, Chris.

II. Title.

332.6324

Cover design by Rob Cowpe

Images on pages 49, 97 and 98 © PhotoDisc, Inc.

Printed in Australia by McPherson's Printing Group

10 9 8 7 6 5 4 3 2 1

Disclaimer

[Contents]

(cont'd...)

How This Book Came About

After writing half a dozen books on investing in the sharemarket —including the bestselling *Top Stocks* and *How the Stock Market Really Works*—I was approached by my publisher and asked if I would write a book explaining how investing in commercial property 'really works'. In other words, it was to be an introductory guide that would take those of you with little or no knowledge of the subject a long way along the path to success, while at the same time acting as a valuable resource for the more experienced investor.

I welcome a challenge, and on first reflection the task seemed easy enough—so I agreed. Besides, I saw it as an ideal way to 'learn on the job' and perhaps it would even enable me to begin my own foray into commercial property investment.

However, as I embarked on the research for this new book, it soon became apparent just how little material there was available. So, I ventured onto the internet, and took a look at what the major national and international real estate companies had to offer.

If you care to take a look, you'll find their websites are quite sophisticated and rather impressive. But, for the most part, the sites are more or less glorified corporate brochures. The principal focus is on promoting their business (and properties) to both the institutional and larger, professional investors, as opposed to assisting the smaller, private investor.

Many of these websites contain a fair amount of in-depth information. But the level of statistical detail left a novice like me somewhat confused, and with little idea as to where the trends and opportunities actually existed within the commercial property market. Nor did the websites lead me through any of the basic steps a beginner needs in order to make a start.

At this point in my search, I came across an Australian website called Gardner+Lang, which is specifically designed to guide the small to medium investor in successful commercial property investment. Gardner+Lang's stated aim is to 'help people who are (or plan to be) high-income or high-net-worth investors … acquire, manage and market commercial property—for maximum return.' And that's just what they do.

Your Gardner+Lang 'education' starts with a free monthly eBulletin, which aims to keep you informed about emerging trends, and lets you know how you can take advantage of the various opportunities. But there is also a whole host of other material, which convinced me I had finally found what I was looking for.

So I picked up the phone and gave Gardner+Lang a call, with two objectives in mind:

➲ getting some personal advice on my own investment requirements

➲ gleaning some much-needed material for my new book.

I wasn't disappointed. Not only did managing director Chris Lang help me acquire a very affordable office investment with attractive depreciation benefits, but I found, to my surprise, that Chris had already written four bestsellers on property investment himself.

Consequently, after three meetings with Chris, I found myself the proud owner of my first commercial property; plus, he had agreed to co-author this new book intended to help you understand *How Investing in Commercial Property Really Works.*

Martin Roth
Melbourne
July 2003

Acknowledgments

It is with much gratitude and thanks that the authors would like to acknowledge the invaluable assistance of the following people:

Janene Murdoch of the Educated Investor Bookshop (www.educatedinvestor.com.au)

Mike Williams of Williams Partners, an accounting firm servicing the specific needs of small to medium businesses and investors (www.wp.com.au)

Nicola Woodward of Apex Property Consulting, a boutique tax-depreciation company (www.apexproperty.com.au)

Craig Boland of Terrain Commercial Loans (www.terrainhomeloans.com)

Your Introduction to Commercial Property

Setting the Scene

Australians have had a long-term love affair with property.

It is a love affair that has often been reciprocal, with property offering great rewards for many. In fact, for plenty of Australians it is the 'investment' in the family home that is the main source of their wealth.

Some have progressed further, building a portfolio of investments in residential properties. The popular strategy has been to buy one or more rental properties in order to provide a tidy retirement income.

Nevertheless, Australians have not generally ventured far into commercial property, despite its many attractions. The big exception has been the Property Trust sector of the stock market, which has seen explosive growth. In addition, certain publicly listed property development companies, like Westfield Holdings and Lend Lease, have provided investors with excellent returns.

But, at the time of writing, we are seeing some changes occur. A weak stock market, fears that residential property prices may well have peaked for a time and a range of new investment opportunities have all combined to move the spotlight onto the 'undiscovered' benefits of commercial property.

You'll quickly find these attractions include high yields (generally far higher than for residential property or the stock market), security of income, tax benefits and the chance of significant capital gain. It is also worth noting that studies have shown commercial property often performs well when other asset classes are weak.

21st Century Trends

Commercial property's attractiveness as a counterbalance to other asset classes was much in evidence during 2001 and 2002, as institutional investors heavily re-weighted their portfolios towards property. Thus, Property Trusts was the best-performing Australian Stock Exchange sector in both years.

There was also a huge inflow of funds into the big public property syndicates for commercial property, which have soared in value to become—in mid-2003—a $9 billion market, up from under $1 billion in mid-1998. Property syndicates typically offer dividend yields of 8 to 10 per cent, and sometimes more.

Another trend of recent years has been a stream of new investment opportunities allowing private investors to put their dollars into highways, airports, health care facilities, retirement property and more.

The result is that some people, realising the high yields of commercial property, and with considerable equity in their homes (thanks to recent rises in values), are starting to borrow in order to invest directly in the commercial property market. Many who have been using gearing strategies to acquire a portfolio of residential property are finding that they can achieve even better returns with commercial property.

How to Get the Most From This Book

You'll find this book has been written for all investors attracted to the market by recent trends emerging in commercial property. It has been divided into three parts:

Part I: The Basics covers what you need to know to get started in commercial property, all the many benefits of such an investment and a lot of data on which type of property would be most appropriate for your needs.

Part II: Direct Property Investment is the main part of the book and covers the process of buying your own investment property in detail. This includes working with property consultants, the eight steps to acquiring a property for maximum return, how to rate investment opportunities, as well as information on financing, taxation and property management.

Part III: Other Property Investments contains three comprehensive chapters on the many opportunities in public property syndicates, listed property trusts and a selection of other investment areas. These chapters introduce you to these investments, highlight their particular attractions—as well as some of their negatives—and explain just how you can get involved.

There are also appendices containing details on where to seek further information, a section on how to conduct successful negotiations and some performance statistics.

You'll find a glossary of technical terms has also been included.

Part I
The Basics

The Attractions of Commercial Property

chapter 1

What Exactly is Commercial Property?

You might be quite surprised, but most Australian investors already 'own' commercial property. They do this through units (shares) in listed property trusts (LPTs), which they have bought directly on the stock market, or simply hold indirectly, usually as part of a superannuation fund.

LPTs (which are examined in greater detail in Chapter 21) invest in shopping centres, office buildings, factories, warehouses and, recently, other assets such as hotels and health care properties.

Even so, local investors have not generally recognised commercial property as a separate asset class distinct from equities and residential property, and often they don't fully appreciate its many attractions. This is rather unfortunate

3

because in many cases, commercial property offers higher returns than other investments, and with less risk—which is why institutional investors have been directing ever-increasing flows of funds towards it in recent years.

Essentially, commercial property is non-residential property. That means it comprises shops, offices, factories, warehouses, hotels, hospitals and the like. For the purposes of this book, agricultural property is excluded. Holiday units, time shares, and so on are also out as these do not relate directly to commercial property. Infrastructure assets—such as highways and airports—are included.

Commercial property can range from the corner milk bar to a giant shopping centre with 100,000 square metres of retail space; from a local accountancy office to a CBD office tower; and from a car repair workshop to a massive steel plant.

But if you have the money, you can buy an office or shop as an investment, in much the same way many Australians buy residential investment property. Indeed, if you have enough money, you can buy a whole block of shops or offices, or even an office tower or an entire shopping centre.

When you purchase property in this way, it is usually known as a 'direct investment'. By contrast, buying units in a property trust is classed as an 'indirect investment'.

Public property syndicates (another means of direct property investment, covered in detail in Chapter 22) have seen a booming inflow of funds in recent years. Even though they are not listed, syndicates have many similarities to property trusts. However, they are usually formed to buy just one property (or, sometimes, several properties) for a fixed period of time.

4

You'll also find several other investment options covered in this book, including:

⊃ property securities funds (unlisted trusts which buy units in a bundle of listed property trusts)

⊃ mezzanine finance

⊃ mortgage trusts

⊃ unlisted property trusts

⊃ direct investment in property company shares.

Influences on Commercial Property

The performance of retail and industrial property has a fairly direct relationship with the state of the economy. As the economy expands, demand for consumer goods increases, and retailers and their suppliers need more (and improved) buildings, factories, shopping centres, leisure facilities and so on. Likewise, an economic downturn can have an adverse impact on this part of the market. The long lead-time associated with office construction tends to make this sector less vulnerable to short-term fluctuations.

Similar to residential property, interest rate levels are also important. As it becomes cheaper to borrow money, clearly there will be more demand for new and existing commercial property.

Government policies—at both the federal and state levels—also have an impact: from property taxes, to zoning, to new environmental regulations.

Other trends are at work as well. Population movements are clearly important: a growing suburb will attract new and upgraded shopping centres and offices, and new highways or rail lines will lead to the creation of fresh business parks.

Technology is also an important factor. Modern office buildings are wired to provide access to the latest telecommunications and hi-tech facilities. Increasingly, tenants expect this. Another trend is towards 'green' buildings, with a particular emphasis on buildings that minimise greenhouse gas emissions.

The Benefits of Commercial Property

As you can imagine, the benefits of commercial property are numerous. For many investors a key attraction of property (and a reason that so many Australians have, over the decades, been happy to invest as much money as possible in property, particularly residential) is that it is actually something tangible. It is there, it's real—you can see and you can touch it.

A piece of land and a building cannot go bankrupt (even if the tenant may). Holders of shares in companies such as HIH Insurance and One-Tel know (all too sadly) that companies can go bankrupt, and the shares suddenly become worthless.

While the value of commercial property can have a direct relationship to the economy, the property is still there, even if the economy takes a nosedive. And while the economy remains firm, commercial property should maintain value—and even appreciate—as well as providing a good income stream.

There are a whole host of other benefits. These include:

➲ strong returns

➲ stability of income

➲ lower risk

➲ exposure to different sectors of the economy

⊃ considerable tax benefits

⊃ hedging against inflation

⊃ investment control

⊃ the ability to add value

⊃ leverage.

These will be looked at individually in the following pages.

Strong Returns

Commercial property, as we shall see throughout this book, provides strong and reliable returns, in the form of income and capital gains. As an investor, you're unlikely to make a quick buck; but over time, you should achieve a return consistently above inflation, at least on a par with residential property and even stock market gains.

It is difficult to get precise figures on the comparative performance of commercial property, due to a lack of standardised benchmarks. Nevertheless, Property Council of Australia figures indicate that, over the 15 years to June 2002, office property realised an average net annual return of 7.8 per cent, with retail property at 12.9 per cent and industrial property at 11.2 per cent.

By comparison, a report commissioned by the Australian Direct Property Investment Association found that, over the same period, Australian shares returned 8.4 per cent, overseas shares 8.1 per cent, managed funds 8.9 per cent, residential property 13.6 per cent and fixed-interest investments 10.7 per cent.

Another report, commissioned by the Australian Stock Exchange itself, found listed property trusts (that is, commercial property) to have been the best performer—of five asset classes —in the 10 years to December 2002 (see figure overleaf).

Figure 1.1: Investment Returns for 10 Years to December 2002

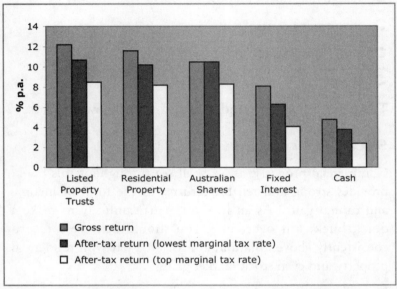

Source: Data derived from Australian Stock Exchange, Towers Perrin.

Stability of Income

One of the important points about commercial property is that not only are the returns generally higher, they are usually more secure. Try to imagine a stock market investment with an 8 or 9 per cent dividend yield. It is likely to be a company for which the share price has plunged—due to a less than rosy outlook—or which is paying a special one-off bonus dividend. The stock market average dividend yield in mid-2003 was around 4.3 per cent. For the Property Trust sector, the average yield was about 7.3 per cent.

Even with residential property, it is difficult to find something offering that kind of rental income—unless you have enjoyed exceptional luck (or skill) in buying cheaply and renting well. As a result of the extended house-price boom, average gross rental yields (from which you have to deduct outgoings such as rates) had fallen to under 4 per cent by mid-2003.

Yet with commercial property, not only are net yields (where your tenant pays the outgoings on top of the rental) relatively high—8 per cent is easily achievable with many property syndicates and direct property investments—they are usually also far more secure.

If you buy shares in a property trust or property syndicate, the chances are that many of the tenants of the relevant properties will be blue chip clients, with long-term leases providing for rental increases in line with inflation. Even if you buy an office or shop yourself as an investment, it is likely that your lease contract will provide for fixed rental increases, or increases in line with inflation. There will likely be provision to recover all the building operating costs, such as rates, insurance, maintenance, air-conditioning running costs and so on.

Unlike residential property (where a lease period of just one year is common), commercial property leases will generally be for a minimum of three years and, sometimes, for five to ten years. Indeed, the anchor tenant in a giant shopping centre will generally have a lease for 15 to 25 years. Some leases incorporate bank guarantees in the event of a tenant's default.

Lower Risk

Commercial property investment will generally carry less risk than residential property or the stock market. A report from the Australian Direct Property Investment Association on

15-year investment returns has measured relative risk, based on a standard deviation volatility formula (the lower the figure, the less risk). The table below illustrates the results.

Table 1.1: **15-year Investment Sensitivity**

Asset Class	Volatility (%)
Cash	1.1
Retail property	2.8
Industrial property	4.5
Composite property	4.9
Fixed interest	5.2
Office property	6.3
Residential property	8.6
Listed property	11.7
Managed funds	12.3
Overseas shares	15.3
Australian shares	18.0

Source: © Australian Direct Property Investment Association (www.adpia.com.au) and Atchison Consultants. Reproduced with permission.

Exposure to Different Sectors of the Economy

A particular attraction of commercial property is that it is possible for you to gain benefit from different parts of the economy. Retail and industrial properties probably have the highest direct relationship to the economy, with retail property dependent on consumer spending trends. Leisure property is influenced by tourism trends and retirement property by the ageing population.

Because commercial property is generally a long-term proposition, few investors would try to move in and out of the various sectors, looking to catch the rises. But for those who believe that, say, the retirement market offers strong potential, commercial property can provide an attractive investment vehicle.

Tax Benefits

You will find that commercial property provides you with generous tax benefits (these are outlined in detail in Chapter 19).

Depreciation allowances on plant and equipment within the building—such as air conditioning, carpets and lighting— are just one benefit. The actual amounts will depend on the value and age of the equipment.

Some properties also attract building allowances, whereby a portion of the structural cost can be offset against assessable income. However, the specific amount varies according to the date of construction and the type of building. You'll learn more about this later.

A Hedge Against Inflation

Many recent years of low inflation may have lulled Australians into a false sense of security about the dangers of rising prices. Yet, historically, this country does not have a good record on inflation.

Property has traditionally been viewed as a good hedge against inflation. Commercial property certainly has an excellent record of outpacing inflation; not only recently (as shown in Table 1.2), but over a long period. The figures are from the Property Council of Australia's Investment Performance Index. A more complete table of these figures is provided in Appendix A.

Table 1.2: Investment Performance Index – Commercial Property

Year Ending	Office* (%)	Retail* (%)	Indust.* (%)	CPI (%)
June 1998	10.5	9.7	15.1	0.7
Dec. 1998	9.9	9.9	15.0	1.6
June 1999	8.9	11.1	14.6	1.2
Dec. 1999	8.5	10.7	13.4	1.8
June 2000	10.0	11.5	12.2	3.2
Dec. 2000	11.0	12.7	12.2	5.8
June 2001	11.0	11.2	12.5	6.0
Dec. 2001	10.0	10.3	12.4	3.1
June 2002	8.6	10.7	11.6	2.8
Dec. 2002	8.0	11.7	12.6	3.0

(* annual return—that is, income and capital gain, minus expenses—
as a percentage of the value of the property.
CPI = Consumer Price Index.)

Source: © Property Council of Australia—Investment Performance Index.
Reproduced with permission.

Investment Control

As an owner of direct property, you have a significant degree of control over your investment, unlike the owners of shares. Of course, some investors (who may have been stung by problems with a poor tenant) prefer the sharemarket for that very reason. But, as some of the recent corporate collapses have demonstrated, major company bosses are not necessarily working in your interests as a shareholder.

Your degree of control can include such aspects as: renovations, upgrading, a change of use of the property, the terms of the lease, the type of tenant, development and disposal.

Adding Value

Though the prime attractions of commercial property include higher yields and stability of earnings, it is possible to further enhance a property's worth by 'adding value'—just as some investors in residential property buy a rundown home for the purposes of renovation. In fact, the opportunities to add value to commercial property are often far greater in number than for residential property. Ways for you to add value to a property include:

- renovating
- upgrading
- subdividing or enlarging
- improving the appearance
- obtaining permission for a redevelopment
- renegotiating the lease
- changing the use.

Leverage

As with residential property, it is possible to borrow against a commercial investment. Depending on your comfort level and financial situation, you could be in a position to control a large number of highly geared properties.

The Negatives of Commercial Property

No investment is risk-free, and commercial property is not necessarily for everyone. Some possible disadvantages are:

- ➲ lack of liquidity

- ➲ lack of pricing information

- ➲ scarcity of other information

- ➲ high cost

- ➲ ongoing management.

These will be looked at individually in the following pages.

Lack of Liquidity

Property trust shares are liquid, and you can buy and sell them readily. Not so for most other commercial property investments.

Property syndicates are generally for a fixed term of at least five years, and it is not generally easy to sell a holding unless you can find a buyer yourself.

A direct property investment can be sold, but, like selling a home, the process can take several months and will incur the normal selling costs. This could prove to be a problem in the event of a severe economic downturn, when you may need to sell a particular property investment as quickly as possible.

With shares, you might simply sell at a greatly depressed price. But with commercial property it could mean months of effort, or even the possibility of you having no buyers at all.

Lack of Pricing Information

Share prices are published every day in your newspaper. Managed fund prices are freely available too. Even average residential property prices for each suburb are published regularly in the real estate sections of newspapers.

But, apart from sales reported in the daily papers, there is little price information available for investors in commercial property. So, you have no real way of knowing just how much a particular investment, other than a property trust, might have changed in value.

It was for this reason that the Property Council of Australia launched its Investment Performance Index for commercial property, measuring income, capital gain and total return. It has become an Australian benchmark, and in late-2002 was based on the performance of nearly $45 billion worth of investment property nationwide.

The index can be broken down in numerous ways, including regional performance figures, though most data is generally available only to subscribers. Some figures have already been provided in this chapter, and more are included in Appendix A.

Scarcity of Other Information

Take an interest in the stock market and you will find a huge amount of investor information—far more than you can reasonably absorb. There are magazines, books, newspaper supplements, seminars, training courses, websites, stockbroking newsletters and reports, and more. Even the residential property investment market is fairly well covered—with books, at least one magazine and regular features in the media.

But as an investor taking an interest in commercial property, you will find little guidance, other than some articles and broking reports on listed property trusts. Some real estate agencies are working to educate new investors with booklets and websites. The Property Council of Australia is working to help investors, with a comprehensive introductory booklet on the subject, titled *Build Your Wealth*, and an informative website (www.propertyoz.com.au).

You'll also find regular reports in the press, particularly in *The Australian Financial Review* and *The Australian*, but you'll discover it is not investor information per se. Rather, this is mainly news about developments in the commercial property market and is aimed at readers who are already participants in the market.

There is a fair amount of data prepared for the property professional, but it is expensive, and is not normally for the novice. A leading data provider is Property Investment Research, which sells newsletters and annual reports. However, to take an example, its *Annual Listed Property Trust Review 2003* sells for $495 (though reduced prices are generally available for private investors).

The fact remains that, as a beginner in the commercial property market, you will really struggle to find enough published data to help distinguish a good investment property from a poor one. (We hope you'll find this book fills part of that gap.)

High Cost

If you have only limited funds for commercial property—a few thousand dollars or less—you will probably lean towards listed property trusts. Property syndicates generally carry a minimum investment amount, usually at least $10,000.

You'll be unlikely to tackle direct property investment with under $100,000, but generally, you'll need much more.

In contrast, with the stock market it is possible to start with a small investment (around $500) and build it up gradually.

Ongoing Management

A direct property investment can require your ongoing involvement with the property. Unless you engage a skilled property manager, you'll need to maintain the property yourself.

You need to be aware of market trends. For example, if you own an office property, it could be that the owners of nearby offices are rewiring their buildings with cabling for high-speed telecommunications. Unless you do the same, your property could become less desirable if the tenant were to vacate.

Also, though lease contracts offer considerable protection, they cannot stop a tenant going bankrupt. That's where the bank guarantee (or bond) from the tenant comes in handy.

All in all, commercial property can seem quite a challenge if you're just starting out. And many of the professionals in this sector of the market are happy for it to remain a mystery to all but a privileged few. Therefore, the purpose of this book is to help 'lift the veil' on these inside secrets of commercial property.

Summary

In this chapter, you have learned of the many benefits of an investment in commercial property (along with the negatives).

You may have been surprised to find that commercial property is so attractive—thanks in particular to high yields and stability of income, along with capital gains. You may even be wondering why you have heard so little about this before. Why is the personal finance media so full of detail on the stock market and residential property investment, with comparatively little on commercial property? This book is intended to fill that gap.

In the next chapter we'll start to outline your investment options, and give you more of the information you need to get started.

Helping You
Make a Start

[chapter 2]

Is Commercial Property for Me?

In Chapter 1 you saw how, if you are an investor, you probably already own some commercial property assets, through listed property trusts. The relevant question is, therefore, do you need more?

As we've discussed, two key attractions of commercial property are the high yield and the security of income. That's why it is especially suitable for retirees and others needing income. It is less appropriate for a high-growth portfolio, which would normally have a hefty exposure to the sharemarket. Nevertheless, its stability makes commercial property an attractive counterbalance to growth assets.

There are also timing considerations. You'll find commercial property is likely to do well when other asset classes are weak.

Your weighting in commercial property should increase at times when the stock market is weak and residential property is looking expensive (as in mid-2003, when this book was being written).

Data company Property Investment Research has recommended that property should form between 10 per cent and 40 per cent of an investment portfolio. In support of a 40 per cent allocation, it wrote:

> Historically direct property returns have moved in a direction which is opposite to those of equities or bonds. The addition of property to a portfolio, predominantly comprising equities and fixed interest, will lower the risk of the total portfolio.

> While being regarded as 'illiquid', property forms 50 per cent of the world's wealth. What proportion of investors really requires more than 50 per cent liquidity in a portfolio?

> Listed property trusts could clearly constitute part of the 40 per cent...

The company also pointed out that listed property trusts consistently outperform equities and have the lowest beta (measure of risk) of the top five industry sectors. Further, Property Investment Research stated that the comparison of property to stocks was not a case of 'apples with apples', citing a difference in gearing (and therefore levels of risk) as a significant difference.

Investment Options

So, what are the investment options available for those interested in commercial property?

Listed Property Trusts

The simplest way to invest in commercial property is through a listed property trust, which involves little more than opening an account with a stockbroker, depositing some money (or linking to a bank account) and then placing an order.

In theory, you can buy as few shares as you wish. In fact, broking fees make it impracticable to buy less than, say, $1,000 worth. Even that amount, with a broking fee of around $30, means you require a return of 3 per cent just to break even.

Property Securities

Property securities are managed funds that invest in a basket of listed property trusts. They are especially suited for the conservative investor unsure about which property trusts are most appropriate. Purchase is through a prospectus.

Public Property Syndicates

Public property syndicate investments are also simple, with application via a prospectus. However, they often require a fairly large minimum outlay, usually of around $10,000. You are then normally locked into the investment for the duration of the syndicate (unless you can find someone willing to buy the investment from you).

Direct Property Investment

Direct property investment is for the person who has researched the market and has acquired some knowledge. You could acquire a property for as little as $100,000, although (as with residential property) that amount wouldn't get you much. From there, you can invest as much as you choose. It is also possible to buy into direct property through a private property syndicate, which we'll cover later.

Mortgage Funds

Mortgage funds are managed funds that lend money over property. They offer the investor security and returns that might be a little higher than a bank term deposit or cash management account, but there is no capital gain.

Mezzanine Finance

Mezzanine finance is the provision of funding for commercial property developments. As the name suggests, it involves providing funds between the developer's own equity and that allocated by mainstream commercial lenders. It thus carries a higher degree of risk—and the potential for higher returns—than regular mortgage finance.

Direct Property Versus Indirect Property

For the purposes of this book, indirect property comprises property trusts. Direct property is a piece of land (usually with a commercial building on it) that you buy yourself. Property syndicates are also classed as direct property.

Most investors assume there is little difference. Indeed, a particular listed property trust and a particular property syndicate may own portfolios of properties that are remarkably similar. Yet the investment performance can be different.

The key point, of course, is that property trusts are listed on the stock exchange, and so are subject to the vagaries of the equity markets. Prices change daily. By contrast, direct property prices are based on expert valuation, and in a time of inflation the appraised value may lag. Listed trusts thus show substantially more volatility than direct property investments, meaning that they carry more risk. One study has shown that listed trust prices can fluctuate by as much as 30 per cent per year, compared to an average annual 8 per cent variation for direct property investments.

On the other hand, listed property is highly liquid, unlike a direct property investment.

You also need to consider timing issues. In an economic downturn, the authorities may lower interest rates and purchase short-term securities, to inject liquidity into the economy. This tends to flow through to the stock market, with a positive impact on listed property trusts, even before the economic recovery has begun.

However, direct property tends to move later in the economic cycle, when a recovery is well under way.

Table 2.1 is based on a study published in *Australian Property Journal*, which tried to determine the correlation between various types of property and other investment sectors. It found the following (where 1 means a perfect correlation and −1 a perfect inverse correlation, with 0 indicating that any correlation is random).

Table 2.1: Correlation Between Property and Other Investment Sectors

ASSET CLASS	CORRELATION WITH PROPERTY
Equities	-0.04
Bonds	-0.25
Listed property trusts	-0.13
Unlisted property funds	0.96

Source: *Data derived from* Australian Property Journal, *May 2002, page 82.*

It is worth noting that, in this study, the performance of an investment in direct commercial property did not have a strong correlation to the performance of listed property trusts, which behaved more closely to equities and bonds.

Where do your Profits Come From?

Investors in commercial property need to understand where their profits come from.

Tenants

In general, the key is the tenants, who provide a steady stream of income. So finding reliable tenants is crucial, which means understanding their needs and providing appropriate property. If you are the owner of a piece of commercial property, it is essential that you know what tenants expect. Also, as good tenants are a crucial part of the profit equation, it is possible to increase the value of the property by changing it in some way —an upgrade, say, or a change of use—in order to attract better tenants.

Leases

The terms of the lease are important. You will find a good lease usually provides for rental increases at least in line with inflation or with economic growth. It may well include conditions that limit rental falls in times of economic downturn. The lease should also include provision for regular rental reviews, with such reviews based on market conditions.

The length of the lease will vary, with smaller premises often attracting shorter lease periods, but the minimum is usually three years. For big office buildings, a typical rent period might be for five to ten years, with an option to renew for a further period. For a large or purpose-built factory, the lease period may be ten years with an option to renew for a further ten.

Capital Gains

The other main source of profit is capital gain. This will not always be as high as can be expected from residential property because the supply and demand equation is different—but the opportunities are there. Just as certain suburbs can go in and out of fashion with homeowners, so can commercial properties in a particular area enjoy greatly increased demand. Thus, shops in a high-growth district could increase in value, while improved transportation facilities can boost the value of factories and offices.

Short-Term Strategies

Commercial property is typically a long-term investment, bought for a high and regular yield. Being somewhat illiquid (except for listed property trusts) generally makes it an asset class that is unsuitable for short-term trading.

Nevertheless, an investor with some knowledge and experience can find properties which can be improved, and then quickly sold for a capital gain. Typically this involves enhancing the income flow of the property, and also the security of the income flow, thus boosting the property's value.

There are various ways to do this. The most basic, of course, is to buy a rundown property and renovate it. An astute investor might also be able to find a property with a lease that does not reflect current rental. Renegotiating the lease could lead to a higher rent, thus boosting the value of the property. Longer leases and better-quality tenants—such as a national supermarket chain—can make a property more valuable.

Some properties have been badly managed. For example, a block of shops might have a vacancy, or tenants who attract little business. Making the shops more appealing to better tenants can bring in higher rents.

Spotting opportunities in growing neighbourhoods, or in neighbourhoods such as inner-city suburbs attracting an increasing number of upmarket residents, is another good short-term strategy.

With experience, you can buy vacant land and develop it, or buy a vacant building and find tenants. Enterprising investors might, with imagination, discover ways to completely change the use of a property—turning a warehouse into a restaurant, for example, could boost its value. (Chapter 16 gives a couple of examples of imaginative property devlopment.)

Timing the market is another viable short-term strategy. As with the stock market, commercial property can go through a lengthy period when values do not change much, followed by a period of sharp appreciation.

Timing and the Commercial Property Cycle

If you are a sharemarket participant, you are likely familiar with the so-called 'investment clock', which purports to show how the economic cycle influences equities.

Thus, an overheating economy is followed by rising interest rates and falling share prices. Then, as the economy declines interest rates start to fall and share prices rise again.

Some analysts have tried to devise a similar 'clock' for commercial property. But unfortunately, the results are not generally useful. Commercial property has so many components, and these do not necessarily move in unison.

For example, industrial property prices may be sagging while retail property prices rise. There are regional differences too. Prices might be hot in Sydney and lukewarm in Melbourne or Brisbane, or vice versa.

Nevertheless, using a highly broad-brush approach, it is possible to place property in the investment cycle thus:

➲ The economy starts to slow.

➲ Direct property prices stop rising, and may decline.

➲ The authorities inject liquidity into the economy.

➲ The stock market and listed property trusts rise.

➲ The economy begins to recover.

➲ Direct property prices start to rise.

➲ Inflation may also rise.

➲ Interest rates rise.

➲ The stock market and listed property trusts fall.

The Four Phases of Commercial Property

American research has tried to identify four phases for commercial property, based on economic and supply–demand factors.

Phase One: This is the bottom of the cycle, and is when the market is generally in a condition of oversupply, due to both a weak economy and too much new construction, from when the economy was still strong. Vacancy rates may be high and rents falling. However, during this period, new construction generally ceases, while demand slowly starts growing again, and the existing oversupply is gradually absorbed.

Phase Two: Demand for new space continues to grow, but with little new construction, rents rise—sometimes sharply. This leads to developers once again initiating the construction of new buildings, until at some point there is rough equilibrium between supply and demand.

Phase Three: Demand continues to rise, but supply is growing faster, and rental growth may slow down.

Phase Four: The market is coming to a point of oversupply, due to over-building, with the condition perhaps aggravated by a weakening economy.

Summary

This chapter should have made you aware of the various investment options that await you. Did you realise the extent of your choices and how easy it is to get started? Now you are ready for an overview of the entire commercial property market.

An Overview
of the Marketplace

chapter 3

Main Investment Sectors

For most investors, commercial property means office, retail or industrial property. However, opportunities exist in other sectors, such as the leisure and retirement sectors, and infrastructure investment is another fast-growing area.

Below is a brief overview of the main investment sectors.

Office Property

In 2003, Australia had an estimated 18 million square metres of office space. About three-quarters of this was in the CBDs, and much of the remainder in a dozen major office locations.

Institutional investors—particularly listed property trusts—own around half of all office property, which makes some of Australia's major building icons accessible to even small investors.

29

You will find that office yields can vary by region. Certain market segments have a concentration in particular cities—government tenants in Canberra, media in Sydney, the financial industry in Sydney and Melbourne, and so on—and this can make for differences in office requirements, in rents and in yields. Growth prospects for each city are also a factor. Figure 3.1 below illustrates the variance of office yields in different regions.

Figure 3.1: Average Initial Yields for Premium Office Property

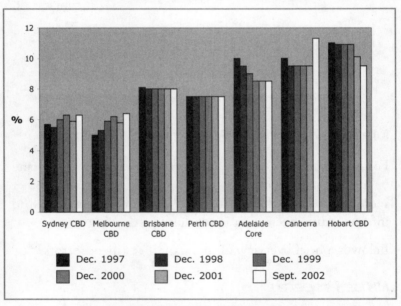

Source: Data derived from Colliers International.

White-collar job growth is a major factor in determining trends in demand for office space. In analysing office property, it is also necessary for you to look at factors such as planned new construction, current vacancy rates, lease terms and rentals.

As an investor interested in office property, you need to be aware of trends in the white-collar world. Increasingly, tenants expect a high-tech infrastructure. There are also moves towards environmentally sensitive 'green' buildings.

Another trend you'll be aware of is 'tele-commuting'—working from home, and communicating with the office by computer. Decentralisation is another issue. Some of the major companies are deciding that they do not need an expensive CBD presence, and are relocating to the suburbs.

With continuing growth in giant shopping centres, you will start to see a trend towards converting smaller suburban strip shopping areas into office property.

Another trend is a burgeoning strata office market (offices in a building that are individually owned by investors), especially in Sydney and Melbourne. This has become a high-growth sub-sector, thanks to swelling numbers of smaller property investors concerned that residential property has become expensive and oversupplied, and a growing number of small business owner–occupiers. Some of the latter are buying their offices through their superannuation funds.

Retail Property

As you will appreciate, the retail sector ranges from the major shopping centres, to strip shopping streets, to the local fish-and-chip shop.

The large shopping centres tend to dominate. In 2003, there were some 900 of them throughout Australia, valued at over $35 billion. More than half were owned by listed property trusts or large public property syndicates, making them accessible to small investors.

A growing Australian economy and strong consumer spending trends mean that the retail sector has shown continually strong growth, and retail property yields have been consistently solid (shown in the table below). Long-term leases employed by most shopping centres ensure that returns have stayed strong, even in times of economic downturn.

Table 3.1: Average Retail Property Yield

Year	Yield (%)
1995	8.4
1996	8.0
1997	7.8
1998	8.1
1999	8.0
2000	8.0
2001	7.6
2002	7.6

Source: © Property Council of Australia—Investment Performance Index. Reproduced with permission.

Lack of suitable development sites in major urban areas means that growth tends to come from expanding existing properties. The shopping centres are also placing a new emphasis on leisure and entertainment facilities, and they are staying open longer.

When analysing a shopping centre, it is important for you to consider the 'anchor' tenants—generally large supermarkets or department stores that attract many customers. It is also necessary to look at lease terms. The quality of centre management, although difficult for an outsider to judge, is also important.

Small retail properties are often attractive to private investors looking to buy a single commercial property asset. So, as with residential property, interest rate trends are a factor.

For investors looking at buying a shop or group of shops, a good location is crucial, and a sound tenant mix is also important.

Industrial Property

Industrial property can range from a local workshop to a major international steel plant or oil refinery. Many are owned by the companies themselves, and the size of the market is undeterminable. A growing number of listed property trusts have been formed to invest in this sector, and institutional investors hold more than $5 billion worth of industrial property.

Yields for industrial property have generally been higher than for other kinds, because many sites are purpose-built for a particular tenant or activity, and it might be difficult to find a replacement tenant. However, this also means that tenants are reluctant to move, as it might be hard for them to find suitable alternative premises. As a result, lease renewals are generally high.

You will soon discover that the performance of industrial property is geared fairly strongly to economic growth, though other factors are at work. New transportation facilities have the potential to make certain industrial property assets more valuable. At the time of writing, there is an established trend to convert industrial property in inner-city areas into housing.

The industrial sector is attractive to many smaller investors looking to buy directly into commercial property, as factorettes generally need little maintenance or ongoing expenditure.

If sufficient care is taken in tenant selection, such properties could well suit the 'let and forget' investor.

Hotels and Leisure Property

Overseas tourists play a major role in the growth of the Australian economy, and domestic tourism is a further important contributor. Nevertheless, it is a volatile business, influenced by global economic conditions, and easily dented by events like a contagious new disease outbreak or a terrorist outrage.

Several listed property trusts specialise in hotels and leisure property. Some property syndicates are also available to the smaller investor interested in this sector.

However, such properties have not been strong performers. A report in 2003 commissioned by the Property Council of Australia noted that investments in hotel properties had underperformed all other types of property investments since 1997, and with generally higher risk. Listed property trusts specialising in hotels had also not done well.

Retirement Property

An ageing population means retirement property has considerable investor potential.

At present, some 2.4 million Australians, around 12.5 per cent of the population, are aged over 65. This number is growing rapidly. The Australian Bureau of Statistics estimates that within 50 years more than 6 million Australians will be over 65, representing more than 24 per cent of the total population.

One of Australia's leading retirement property finance specialists, Adelaide Bank, forecasts that the Australian retirement facility population will rise from 120,000 in 2003 to 180,000 by 2011 and 300,000 by 2031.

Until recently, there were few opportunities for investors (apart from buying shares in a small number of publicly listed retirement property developers), but this is changing. Some developers are selling individual units to investors, who generally lease them back to the developer–operator.

The first listed property trust covering this sector, Village Life Property Trust, was launched by Westpac Funds Management in 2003.

Infrastructure

Until recently most infrastructure assets—highways, airports, ports, power plants and so on—were owned by government. However, the politics of economic rationalism has led to a stream of new projects being placed in private hands, along with the privatisation of many public assets. The result is a new wave of investment opportunities in infrastructure property.

Australia has a sophisticated system—ahead of most other countries—of developing so-called BOOT (build, own, operate, transfer) projects, by which the private sector takes on a major development, with the asset eventually transferring to the public sector. This can involve extremely complex risk analysis and financial schemes.

An example is the M2 motorway, linking Sydney's northwestern suburbs with the Pacific Highway. This was developed by the listed company Hills Motorway, which now operates it.

Another example is Melbourne's 22-kilometre CityLink toll road, joining the CBD with northwestern and southeastern suburbs. This $1.2 billion project was undertaken by the private sector and is now operated by the publicly listed Transurban Group.

The huge costs of a project mean that infrastructure companies typically have very high debts. During the construction phase they have little income, so may be unable to pay out anything to their shareholders. Further, during the initial period of operations, heavy debt repayments might limit dividends. But subsequently, companies should enjoy high revenues, and be able to pay a steady stream of dividends.

By their nature, infrastructure assets usually operate in a monopoly, or highly protected, environment, providing essential services. As long as the economy remains firm, it is reasonable to expect that their revenues will be maintained, on a fairly predictable basis. In fact, they should grow, along with the economy, while the ability to pay strong dividends should be enhanced by steady debt repayments.

Like property trusts, infrastructure properties can make excellent investments for those looking for a steady stream of dividends with a relatively low level of risk. There is also the prospect of some capital gain, as the economy grows and also as the company diversifies into other projects. However, due to their heavy borrowings, the companies can be vulnerable to interest rate rises.

Other Opportunities

As commercial property becomes more attractive to small investors, you'll find many more opportunities will present themselves.

Health care and child care properties are examples. With specialised knowledge you can buy a suburban doctor's surgery or a child care centre as an investment. Hospital and medical trusts are also coming. For example, Australian Unity manages the unlisted Healthcare Property Trust, and Peppercorn Management Group has launched the publicly listed Peppercorn Investment Fund, which specialises in child care facilities.

Strata title parking spaces in multistorey parking developments are a niche investment that can provide solid returns for modest outlays. They require minimal upkeep (given that they are leased to the parking building operator) and as they are often in prime locations they offer the potential of eventually being sold at a capital gain for redevelopment.

Looking to the future, long-term storage facilities are as yet a tiny, but growing, property business in Australia, though not in the United States—where several self-storage real estate investment trusts are listed on the stock exchange. An article in *Property Australia* journal in October 1998 quoted the executive officer of the Self Storage Association of Australasia:

> Americans regard self storage as an absolute blue chip investment and it is considered the safest real estate–based investment in the United States.

Summary

Commercial property is normally taken to refer to office, retail and industrial assets. However, as an investor you need to be aware of a fast-growing stream of other options. Tourism and leisure properties are just one example. Health care, child care and retirement properties are blooming into another large sub-sector. An expanding number of infrastructure projects are also opening to the small investor.

This is the end of Part I of the book. Now it's time to make an in-depth examination of all your options in direct property investment.

Part II
Direct Property
Investment

Widening Your
View of Things

As you're aware, this is a book all about commercial property. But, in order to introduce you to several key concepts, you may find it helpful to return to a familiar comfort zone—which is ... buying a residential property. You see, by fully understanding these concepts, they will stand you in good stead as you embark upon your 'new career' as a commercial property investor. Perhaps an example will help to explain things best.

Most people investing in property seem to get 'bent out of shape' about the price. But the price should not be your only consideration. What is vital is *how much a property costs you*, and this means considering more than just the final price paid.

Often, if you allow the vendor to win on price, you can get a better deal overall. Here's a simple lesson that co-author Chris Lang learned during the early 1980s. He has used it repeatedly ever since. It illustrates many of the principles of successful real estate investing.

Controlling the Terms

A young engineer attended one of my property seminars and came up to me afterwards, saying: 'I've found a five-bedroom house in Burwood, and I want to buy it.'

I said: 'How much do you think it's going to bring?'

'About $65,000.'

'How much have you got?'

He replied: '$9,000.'

I said: 'You haven't really got enough, have you?'

To which he replied: 'Well, no. But I've arranged a first mortgage of $45,000, and my mother will help me with the rest.' So we went to the auction, at three o'clock on a Saturday afternoon. And the property was passed in to us at $58,000.

I said to the auctioneer: 'Look, would the vendor take $59,000?'

'No,' said the auctioneer. 'She wants $65,000.'

I said: 'I can probably get my fellow up to $60,000.'

'No,' he replied. 'It's $65,000.'

'What if I can get him up to $61,000? And even that might be difficult, because he's running out of money. Do you think she will take it?'

The auctioneer said: 'Look, she's 90 not out, and she wants $65,000.'

So my client and I went down the street a little way to plan our next step. When we returned, I asked the auctioneer if the old lady might leave some money in the deal, and he went off to ask her. He came back and said: 'She'll leave in $5,000, at 15 per cent.'

You might not believe this now, but back in the early 1980s first mortgage rates were running at 17 per cent, and second mortgage rates were at 22 per cent. So I said to my client: 'I suggest we ask her to leave in $20,000 on second mortgage for three years at 10 per cent.'

In disbelief, he said: 'Do you really think she'd come at that?'

I replied: 'Well, if she only leaves in $15,000, you'll just have to use the $9,000 cash that you've already got. And if she increases from 10 per cent to 12 per cent or even 15 per cent on second mortgage, it is still very cheap second-mortgage finance.'

We made the offer and, to my client's intense surprise, she accepted it. I said to my client, the young engineer: 'You'd have to be pretty happy. You've got your $45,000 first mortgage. You've got your $20,000 second mortgage. And you've still got your $9,000 in the bank!'

Understanding What Went On

This all involved an understanding of people's needs. You see, the vendor was 90 years of age, and I reasoned that she wanted enough money so that she could arrange to go into a retirement home. Therefore, we probably didn't have to give her all the money. We gave her $45,000, and asked her to leave in $20,000.

The second issue was that she had obviously told her relatives she was going to get $65,000. She had achieved this—she didn't have to tell them that she left in $20,000 on second mortgage to get the $65,000. She could simply say: 'There you are. I stood out for it, and got my $65,000.'

The third issue was her willingness to accommodate the 'creative finance' proposal, because she would probably not be around when the other $20,000 came due anyway—this would be her family's concern.

Then, on the following Tuesday, the old lady's lawyer telephoned me with some concerns about the second-mortgage deal. I started to explain that it had been carefully worked out and written down, and everyone seemed quite happy with it.

'No,' he said. 'You don't understand. The interest rate of 10 per cent is going to cause the old lady a problem with her pension. Do you mind if we drop it to 8 per cent?'

You Always Need to Make It a Win–Win Solution

Everyone has to walk away from a deal having felt they've won something. If the old lady had felt hard done by, she would never have come back to us to drop the interest rate to 8 per cent. But she got the $45,000 she needed to go into the retirement home and she had income from the interest—albeit at a lower rate, because that suited her pension situation. She was happy.

My client was happy too. The negative cashflow was not a problem for him because, as an engineer, he was on a good salary. And as he wasn't married, he was able to let out the other four bedrooms to generate more income.

So remember: you can let the vendor name the price, but you can name the terms.

Summary

As you probably appreciate, there were a fair number of real estate principles wrapped up in this one deal. And we shall be developing these as we go along in the remainder of this section of the book.

In the next chapter, we'll introduce you to some of the emerging trends in commercial property.

Emerging Trends in Commercial Property

One of the keys to success in property investment is staying abreast (and ideally, ahead) of trends in the market. This particularly involves being aware of which areas of the market are doing well now, which are performing poorly, and which have the potential to boom.

It means you need to read widely on the topic. Appendix B is your 'resource centre', which provides extensive detail on the main sources of information on commercial property that are currently available to the investor. These include selected websites that you should consult regularly, along with newspapers and specialist journals.

When the Market Goes Against You

Too many investors become discouraged when the market turns down, not realising that it could actually be a buying opportunity. We saw this in the last downturn, in the early 1990s, when many people became confused about what to do.

But this can be a time when vendors are keen to do deals. During such a time, if you have the available funds and the advance knowledge, you clearly have a strategic advantage and could therefore be able to buy very well. In addition, you will avoid being caught up in all the hype of a rising market when you make your purchase, and be able to properly analyse a good selection of properties that may remain unsold after auction.

The Property Market in the First Decade of the 21st Century

Though precise figures are not available, several analysts say that, historically, the Australian office property cycle runs for about 18 years from peak to peak, with smaller highs and lows within that cycle. The last high point was in 1989, which suggests that the next peak will be around 2007.

By contrast, the residential property cycle tends to run for five to seven years, and is the market most influenced by external stimuli, such as interest rates and government incentives to first home buyers. The retail and industrial sectors generally fall somewhere in between.

Gardner+Lang's client newsletters at the turn of this century warned that a 'short and sharp' economic downturn was on the horizon, based on a range of unrelated, non-fundamental causes such as the GST and Y2K concerns, consumer sentiment and a post-Olympics building slowdown. Gardner+Lang advised clients to use this period as a window of opportunity for expanding their commercial property holdings, before a likely surge in the market from around mid-2003.

The downturn duly came—short and sharp—and from mid-2003 we are starting to see the commercial property market improve Australia-wide. What are some of the trends that investors can expect over the next few years? A report from economic forecasters BIS Shrapnel in mid-2002 (and again more recently in April 2003) declared the Australian economy to be generally in good shape. Although external factors—including a global slowdown and a rising dollar—might constrain our growth, the construction and commercial property markets are emerging from cyclical downturns, and are ready to rise again in coming years.

Spotlighting the Melbourne office property market, the report said that forecasts of a growing number of new construction projects and of looming oversupply were wrong. It said that metropolitan Melbourne could easily absorb 1.4 million square metres of net additions to stock over 10 years—including 560,000 square metres in the CBD alone—without oversupplying the market.

According to a BIS Shrapnel report, Melbourne could easily absorb 1.4 million square metres of net additions to stock— including 560,000 square metres in the CBD alone— over 10 years without oversupplying the market.

As a result, it expected growth in prime gross effective rents in the CBD market to be some 39 per cent, from 2003 to a peak during 2007.

Decide on Your Strategy and Take Action

The office, industrial and retail property cycles are starting to move together, as they did in the late 1980s, with the makings of a commercial property boom. Usually the best strategy is to acquire your commercial investment properties before the market starts to take off; otherwise you'll get caught up in the hype, when overall investor sentiment starts to rise again. If you buy while many property investors remain pessimistic or somewhat confused, and make sure you cash in your investments before the peak, just imagine the absolute bargains you'll be able to snare with your significantly increased net worth in the trough of the next market cycle.

If you do not sell at or around the market peak, you could suffer the same dramatic losses that investors suffered from 1990 to 1994. And, as those who experienced it will tell you, there was 'blood on the streets'. It was painful for investors to watch sizeable fortunes simply vanish.

You may feel that owning investment property for only a few years sounds like a rather short period. However, if you get your timing right, you'll be doing so at the end of the cycle, when the greatest growth generally occurs.

For each of their clients, Gardner+Lang likes to prepare a projected, after-tax cashflow for the investments they wish to acquire. At the time of writing, these cashflow projections are indicating returns of 12 per cent to 21 per cent per annum (depending upon gearing levels) on the equity you invest.

For the Longer-Term Investor

Not every commercial property investor wants to sell after just a few years, even if numerous indicators are warning of a peak and a subsequent fall. If your investment horizon is, say, 15 years or so, you don't need to pay as much attention to the shorter term trends in the property market.

Nevertheless, the experience of Gardner+Lang is that many clients are currently positioning themselves to sell before an anticipated peak in 2007. They then intend to stay out of the market for about 12 to 18 months, before picking up some real bargains after the market sharply declines. These will be holdings that they will retain for the long term, having bought them at the bottom of the next cycle.

We will now look at trends in office, industrial and retail property.

Office Property

Had it not been for the large amount of suddenly vacated office space following the dot-com sector's decline and September 11, you would have seen CBD office property further ahead than it is at the moment. Indeed, until 2003 it was generally moving sideways, with the leasing market rather soft. However, this was caused by a fall-off in overall demand from new tenants, rather than an oversupply of space from new construction.

Some pundits, particularly in the daily papers, have expressed concerns about a looming oversupply. We do not see this eventuating. You see, unlike the speculative activity of the 1980s, this time new construction is not occurring without a significant pre-commitment. Thus, we think it more likely that rents and values will improve strongly.

For example, in Melbourne, where the construction cycle has started first (other cities have yet to fully start a new development phase at the time of writing), five major new office buildings commenced construction with an overall tenancy pre-commitment of around 50 per cent. These are now over 85 per cent leased, even though they will not be completed until 2005–06. By contrast, in the 1980s, developers simply built new office towers, anticipating that tenants would just turn up.

Another blossoming trend is the development of the suburban office market, which is quite distinct from the CBD. Recently there has been considerable demand for strata offices, with many early retirees, and those with healthy redundancy packages, looking to set up an office close to home in order to launch their own small one- or two-person business.

Industrial Property

Industrial property can range from a local workshop to a major international steel plant or oil refinery, from warehouses to research facilities.

Historically, the fortunes of industrial property tend to follow that of the economy, being reasonably dependent upon consumer spending and, to a lesser degree, export strength. And though our own economy remains generally firm, the global situation will have an impact and could slightly delay the upswing for industrial property.

Nonetheless, as business confidence and investment return, and the office market starts to surge, industrial property will not be far behind. You will start to see a demand for industrial properties with a high office content; this will create competition from commercial developers and investors for the traditional business park locations.

Another trend is that many industrial tenants have suddenly found themselves with enough borrowing capacity—thanks to low interest rates—to actually purchase factories and warehouses for their businesses.

And, with retail sales up, demand for industrial output has risen significantly, causing many industrial tenants to move to newer and bigger premises. That, in turn, puts pressure on rentals, and also makes owner–occupation attractive, especially while interest rates remain low.

As a new wave of building gets under way, you should start to see strong growth in rentals, due to both increased demand and the higher cost of construction.

Generally, the best buys will be in the $2 million–plus range; if you can muster this amount, this is one sector you should certainly consider.

Retail Property

Like industrial property, retail is closely linked to economic conditions. It also shares some similarities to residential property, in that it is sensitive to interest rate movements.

It is well-known that consumer spending has been growing for some years. However, this is not being reflected evenly across all sectors of the market. For example, the household goods sector has boomed as a result of low interest rates and the first home buyers' scheme. In any case, increased sales do not necessarily mean increased profitability.

Recent property sales (reflecting yields as low as 3 to 4 per cent) would tend to confirm investors' perceptions that there is a growing preference by many shoppers for strip centres, as opposed to regional and sub-regional centres. However, the increasing numbers of bulky-goods stores and factory outlets could have a moderating influence on future growth prospects for retail investors.

[Summary]

In this chapter, we have tried to outline some of the trends supporting our view that now is an opportune time to be moving into commercial property.

Historically, the Australian office property cycle runs for about 18 years, from peak to peak. The last high point was in 1989, which suggests that the next peak will be around 2007. We also see growing strength in retail and industrial property, and values often appreciate the most in the last years of the cycle.

In the next chapter we'll help you formulate your own investment strategy.

You Need a Clear Investment Strategy

chapter 6

Creating a Blueprint for Your Future

One of the key objectives of this book is to expand your thinking about the property market, and to help you adopt a new mindset towards what's really going on.

So, in this chapter, we are seeking to give you the ability and the confidence to develop your own investment strategy.

However, if you're like many property investors, you could well be wondering: 'Where do I start?' and 'How do I decide what's right for me, when there are so many exciting opportunities available?' Both of these are good questions. So, let's walk you through the thought process, to help you in arriving at your core area of focus.

You may consider this chapter somewhat 'philosophical'. But it's intended to encourage you to think about commercial property investment in new ways, before you actually start. By contrast, subsequent chapters get down to the 'nuts and bolts' of practical investing.

Distilling Your Personal Investment Strategy

The reason we've explored a number of emerging trends with you is to give you some insight into just what new, moneymaking options you do have available. And with those insights, you're certainly able to hit upon several more property investment opportunities yourself.

You First Need to Consider What's Possible

By now, you have a whole range of potential avenues (or options) there in front of you. And maybe you could depict them in a simple diagram, where the circle below contains all your options, as to *what's possible*.

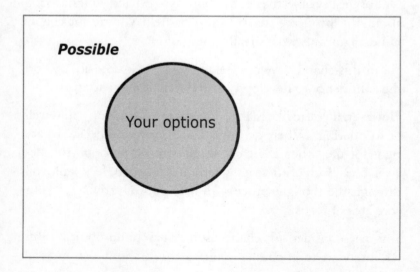

However, at the moment, creating your personal investment strategy may seem like a somewhat daunting task—only because your choices simply appear to be too many.

Let's Now Take a Look at What's Appropriate

You know what's possible, and you need somehow to trim your choices a little. And you can do this by asking yourself: 'Which of the various available options would best fit my temperament?'

Just because an investment option may look appealing, this, by itself, is not necessarily a sound basis for you to pursue it.

For example, in the 1970s and 1980s, negative gearing was being heavily promoted as providing excellent tax benefits. But the problem people had was: 'How much should I borrow?' You see, there's no right answer to that question—it's simply what is right for you. For some people, to borrow 90 per cent of the cost of their investment is fine. But for others, a borrowing ratio of anything over 50 per cent of the cost would cause them considerable distress.

Therefore, you needed to discover what we'll call your 'threshold of insomnia'. And in doing so, you then start to form a clearer view of the type of investments you ought to be including within your portfolio.

That doesn't mean you cling blindly to past choices, where you may intuitively feel most comfortable. But by introducing the concept of what's appropriate, you're able to start narrowing down your newly-found options.

When you start to compare what you consider to be appropriate investments against your possible property investment opportunities, you're then able to trim your choices down to something a lot more manageable.

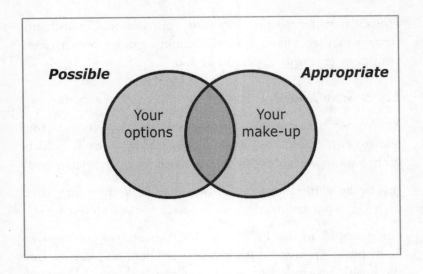

But What Are You Capable of Buying?

You now need to have a look at exactly what your resources might be—both financially and time-wise. And that doesn't mean that you are confined to looking just by yourself. You may like to think about joining with other like-minded investors in a syndicate, to leverage your capital, and spread your risk.

Certainly, as your portfolio grows, you will (like most serious investors) need to engage professional property management expertise, so as not to spread yourself too thin, and then run yourself ragged.

But, assuming that for the time being you have chosen to invest on your own, you then need to properly assess your available capital, which will be a combination of your present cash, plus any additional equity you may have in other properties. And so, your diagram now looks something like the one opposite.

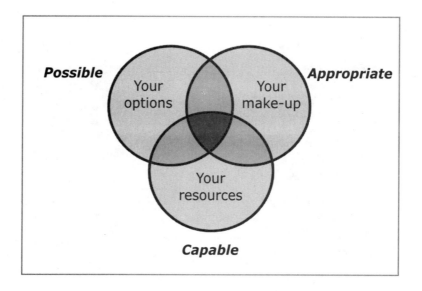

You Need to Establish Your Core Area of Focus

As you can see, after applying these three 'filters', you are left (at the centre of these overlapping circles) with what's *possible*, what's *appropriate* and what it is you're actually *capable* of investing in. Only then are you ready to start building your property wealth.

Contrary to popular opinion, the smaller your list of potential opportunities, the clearer and more successful your investment strategy is likely to be. It's really quite a simple process; but one intended to help you carefully establish your core area of focus! And it's the process even seasoned investors go through from time to time—just to ensure they keep themselves on track.

[Summary]

This chapter has put the spotlight on the importance of you having a clear investment strategy, to enhance your success as an investor in commercial property. In particular, it is crucial that you are able to understand your own temperament. A certain property may look attractive and be available and affordable, but that's not to say it is appropriate for you.

What is your threshold of insomnia? Too many investors rush into an acquisition, perhaps pressured by some hard-talking sales executives, only to find themselves suffering later from sleepless nights.

In the next chapter, you will discover the eight key steps to acquiring an investment property.

Eight Steps for Maximum Returns

[chapter 7]

Don't you find it fascinating that so many people consider themselves to be experts in property—simply because they are surrounded by it? Yet, when you actually quiz them about the investment process involved, you often find their confidence to be quite misplaced.

In this chapter, we are going to take a look at the eight important steps in the process of acquiring an investment property.

Setting the Scene for Success

Just because they live in a house or apartment, work in an office, shop or warehouse, and maybe own a holiday house, many people somehow believe that they automatically have all the knowledge and skills they need to become an expert in most forms of property.

But this might be far from the reality. So, the purpose of this chapter is to help ensure that you fully understand the investment process. Some of what we cover here you will probably know already; but some you may not. Either way, it will give you a handy framework within which to organise the knowledge and skills you have.

Anyway, let's make a start.

Step 1: Gaining the Knowledge You Need, Quickly...

Whether it is property, shares or collectables, you will find successful investment is simply a combination of knowing your options, understanding your risk profile and recognising your constraints, in order to arrive at what we call your core area of focus. (This was covered in some detail in the last chapter.)

As part of the process, you need to quickly acquire the required level of knowledge and experience. Unfortunately, this is easier said than done. There is a huge amount of material available for the beginner investor in shares and in residential property but an amazing dearth for beginners in commercial property.

Some of those in the industry, along with some serious professional investors, obtain a degree in property, which will take you three years of full-time study, and involves a wide range of subjects. These include: macroeconomics, commercial and property law, accounting, valuation principles, statistics, business computing, commercial building, business finance, urban economics, business forecasting, marketing principles, asset management, business research, property investment, property development, urban valuations and more.

So, if you want to fully grasp the 'knowledge' part of successful property investing, that is the extent of what you will need to study. And once you've gained your knowledge base, you then need to marry that with years of practical experience, to make sure you are able to take full advantage of what the market has to offer.

We see this book as an important first step in the path to quickly acquiring the knowledge you need. In particular, the Resource Centre, in Appendix B, directs you to a wide variety of further information sources you can explore.

In fact, many serious commercial property investors leave the necessary, in-depth knowledge to their consultants (see Chapter 9 for more detail on working with consultants), and simply focus upon gaining as much practical experience as they can.

Step 2: Researching the Market

The internet has become a key tool for investors looking to uncover commercial property opportunities. You can read a lot more about this in Appendix B. Sites we find particularly useful include:

➲ Property Look (www.propertylook.com.au)

➲ property.com.au (www.property.com.au)

➲ realestate.com.au (www.realestate.com.au).

Most real estate agents also have their own websites nowadays.

Step 3: Choosing the Right Property

Given the wide range of properties you may have to choose from, you need to adopt some strict guidelines. By doing that, you will both simplify your decision-making process and bring some consistency to the choices you end up making.

In other words, you need an easy-to-use framework around which to source and filter the available properties. To ease this process, we detail in subsequent chapters some sound investment objectives, along with 12 buying criteria. By returning to these two checklists each time you seek to make a purchase, you will probably avoid most of the common pitfalls of property investment.

Step 4: Analysing Your Selection

Sometimes this can prove to be the most confusing and frustrating part of the entire investment process. You have identified a number of properties which seem to fit your objectives and criteria, but you lack a quick and easy method of reducing them down to a workable short-list.

In Chapter 13, we present a method to help you in rating your investment opportunities. It simply combines your objectives and criteria into a compact matrix, allowing you to rate each of your candidate properties in less than a minute. From there, you need to create a projected (4- to 10-year) after-tax cashflow for each property. This is really a job for a professional, unless you have financial analysis skills or the requisite sophisticated computer software.

The cashflow projection would take into account things like:

- ➲ purchase price
- ➲ acquisition costs
- ➲ borrowings
- ➲ interest costs
- ➲ net rental
- ➲ depreciation

- anticipated sale price
- capital gains tax
- selling costs.

Creating cashflow projections is something that some property consultants or financial advisers would do for you as a matter of course, before you make your final decision to acquire a property. Then, using those projections, you can create a common yardstick—the *internal rate of return* (the anticipated, after-tax percentage return on the actual equity you invest)—for each property.

Step 5: Arranging Your Finance

When buying commercial property, you really need to have your finance in place before you put forward any purchase proposal. Or, at least, have the assurance that you're likely to gain approval from your finance source.

You may already have an existing relationship with one or more banks (as most people do). And, given your long-standing relationship (not to mention the numerous titles of yours they may already hold), they'll not only look after you, but also offer you the best deal. Right?

Maybe! But that's not necessarily the case. Gardner+Lang have had clients who seem to trust their banks implicitly to 'do the right thing' by them. We try to suggest that they talk with various finance brokers we've recommended to several of our other clients. But invariably there are some clients who believe they know best.

There was one particular client who, somewhat reluctantly, agreed to explore alternatives through one of these finance brokers. But he still insisted that what his bank was offering him couldn't be bettered.

Not only did we manage to obtain a better rate and better terms, but it was done through his very own bank.

How is that possible?

It's quite simple, really. The broker was able to introduce the prospect of competition for that client's bank.

The client himself didn't feel he was in a position to 'threaten' his own bank. But the broker was able to allude to the possibility of having to relocate all the client's business to another financier, if that's what it took to ensure the client received the best deal for his latest acquisition. Amazingly, the original bank found a way to restructure the finance proposal much more favourably. And the client–banker relationship remained fully intact.

So, you see, arranging finance is more than just taking out a loan. And you'll explore that further in Chapter 14.

Step 6: Negotiating the Deal

You've just read about one of the more common negotiating ploys, which can be used to your advantage. There are lots more. You will find Chapter 15, and also Appendix C, 'How to Negotiate Your Way to Success', will give you more extensive details on negotiating success.

Step 7: Managing Your Property for Profit

There's an old saying: 'You don't make your profit when you sell a property, you make it when you buy it!' And to a large extent that is true. However, you can buy a property very well, but then manage it extremely poorly, and lose a lot of money in the process.

If you do attempt to manage a commercial property yourself, you need to develop a detailed knowledge base in areas such as tenancy law, statutory regulations and construction. And one of the key areas of extreme exposure for landlords is in the Essential Services Regulations—legislation governing monitored services within a property, including air conditioning, fire services, lifts and electrical equipment. Noncompliance will attract significant fines for you, the owner. With so many new changes, this is an area fraught with a diverse range of potential penalties.

That is why most active property investors choose to have their properties professionally managed. See Chapter 20 for more on this topic.

Step 8: When it Comes to Marketing...

You may have bought well. And the property has been skilfully managed. But it's an innovative and highly professional marketing campaign that will put the 'icing on the cake', and help you release the maximum profit from your investment.

That is why it is so important that you exercise wisdom when selecting an agent or consultant to market the property for you, because not all agents are abreast of the trends in marketing properties in the 21st century.

What criteria should you use to select your agent or consultant? We suggest that you visit the agents' websites. Virtually every commercial property agent in Australia is now online. But don't simply judge the sites from how attractive they look. Instead, check on the depth of information that is provided to you— the investor—on details other than simply the properties that are being advertised.

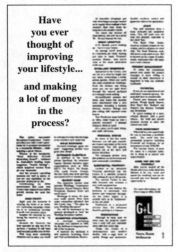

A copy-intensive, quarter-page ad in the daily media for an out-of-town reception centre. Note the compelling headline.

Whether it is using press advertising, direct mail or fliers, promoting a property plays a vital role in the marketing process.

Advertising experts will tell you: 'If you can entice people to read the first 50 words ... then, they will go on to read the next 500.'

The more you 'tell' people, the easier it becomes for you to 'sell' to them. Generally, people like to be educated—which involves copy-intensive advertisements, brochures, direct mail letters and web pages. And so, often the best promotional material looks rather like editorial copy, and is intended to be a pleasurable read (even though it must, of course, be clearly labelled as advertising).

Just think about it for a moment. When you purchase a newspaper, do you buy it mainly for the ads? Probably not. Instead, you buy it for the news and editorial content—which gets you involved, and holds your interest.

Something else we have learned over the years is that often (and it's only afterwards that we find out) many purchasers were not actually looking to buy a property at the time they saw a particular advertisement, or received a letter. So, by using an editorial style, you can hold people's attention long enough to have them start reading what they initially view as 'editorial', or a personal letter.

Anyway, you'll learn more about selling your investment property in Chapter 17.

[Summary]

These eight steps are important. Let's repeat them here:

1. Gaining the knowledge you need.

2. Researching the market.

3. Choosing the right property.

4. Analysing your selection.

5. Arranging your finance.

6. Negotiating the deal.

7. Managing your property for profit.

8. Marketing your property.

In Chapter 8, you'll start to put these procedures to good use, as we prepare you for the purchase.

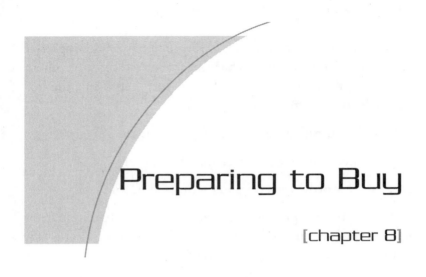

Preparing to Buy

Make Your Plan and Stick to It

As an individual investor, you need to decide exactly what your principal aims are:

- ➲ To earn a good cashflow?

- ➲ To provide a profitable overall yield? Note that a high initial yield often means limited capital gain. Overall yield is a combination of income and capital gain.

- ➲ To benefit from tax savings? As highlighted in Chapter 19, depreciation allowances on new or newly renovated properties can bring significant tax benefits.

- ➲ To hedge against inflation? This is where a high initial yield is sacrificed for longer term capital growth.

Your aim may be to achieve all four objectives, although one or two of them are likely to be more important than the others. And you must be convinced that property represents the best vehicle for maximising your wealth.

Two of your fundamental concerns will be to:

1. protect the original investment; and then

2. get a worthwhile, ongoing return on it.

If these are your principal concerns, then they tend to narrow down the investment alternatives available to you. That is why it is crucial to make a plan. And stick to it.

Your Investment Approach

Your next step is to determine your personal approach to investing. You will find investors normally fall into three categories:

1. The first type are those who love to tell stories about how they 'gambled the lot', knowing that they would either go broke or make a fortune. Such people are fun to listen to, but dangerous to imitate. Remember: if you go for broke in your investment program you stand a good chance of ending up broke.

2. The second type are the armchair investors who always talk a good line. They attend a number of seminars and can answer most technical questions about property and the economy, but they never quite develop the courage to have a go. They prefer the safety of the bank account to the risks of real estate.

3. The third type are the mildly aggressive investors, who increase the size of their portfolio only when they have sufficient funds in reserve. They cover most of the reasonable expenses that go with a new purchase without putting their existing properties at risk. These careful, mildly bold investors are the ones most likely to succeed.

Creating the Right Mindset

The first thing you should do is to draw up a statement of position —a list of all your assets (things like your house, car, shares and other investments) and liabilities (loans, credit cards and other debts)—which tells you exactly what your net worth is.

You see, if you're planning to invest $200,000, you might suddenly say to yourself: 'That's a hell of a lot of money.' But if you prepare a statement of position, you might well find that you are actually worth $1 million—your home, your weekender, your cars, your boat, your furniture and pictures, your insurances and your cash.

Most people are worth more than they realise. So $200,000 is only one-fifth of your net worth. If you lost it all, it wouldn't completely wipe you out. Not that this is even likely—the point is that you need the correct frame of mind to extract the most out of property investment. To do this you must assess your overall financial position, not just the purchase you are considering.

Your Profile as an Investor

If someone is looking to invest under $1 million, we tend to think of them as an 'amateur investor'—they have the money, but probably don't know all that much about real estate to necessarily make a wise decision. Once you go over $1 million, you are usually talking about people who either trade in real estate or who invest long term; they often have another source of income, generally at a corporate level.

Normally, cash funds of about $100,000 put investors into the residential real estate category—although, for the same price, you can certainly find some exciting office suites (often with a three-year income guarantee), where the tenant pays your outgoings for you.

In the commercial category, anyone with under about $500,000 faces a lot of competition. However, as you'd expect, once investors have over $1 million, the range of options opens up considerably.

Hazards You Need to Avoid

You need to recognise that in all investments there are risks. In real estate, your three major pitfalls are:

1. Over-borrowing—that is, borrowing beyond your comfort level.

2. Poor assessment of the market.

3. Buying property with fragile tenants.

Twelve Good Rules You Should Follow

As you'll appreciate, it is important for you to stay just below what we've affectionately called your 'threshold of insomnia'. This is the point at which you start to lose sleep—perhaps through over-borrowing, or making a poor assessment of the market.

Below are a dozen 'dos and don'ts' which seem to have stood the test of time:

1. Do maintain sufficient cash reserves, in order to cover several months' mortgage repayments if you lose a tenant, or the tenant is late in paying. Nothing cures investment insomnia faster than having enough cash to meet any planned and unplanned obligations. And keep a sharp eye on smaller items, like any equipment and maintenance bills, which can quickly add up.

2. Do make an investment plan with which you feel comfortable and then follow it—set achievable goals and go after them. More goals have been missed through lack of planning than through actual failure of a plan.

3. Do get a good financial calculator or software program, and learn to use it properly.

4. Do keep up your pursuit of knowledge—monitoring the news and legislation affecting real estate, attending seminars, staying up with current trends. Knowledge can minimise your risks and maximise your profits.

5. Do retain—and retain means pay fees to—a top property consultant and a competent property lawyer. The money you pay should be more than returned to you in the deals they'll pull off for you.

6. Do avoid personal liability on mortgages wherever possible—try to make the property your sole security.

7. Do commit only a small part of your funds to speculative investments. They may appear glamorous on the way in, but they are often painful on the way out.

8. Do not make deals on a handshake—put them in writing.

9. Do not go into joint ventures or partnerships without deep consultation with your retained advisers.

10. Do not commit funds from the sale of one property to finance another, until they are fully realised. Many 'sure deals' have an uncanny habit of not coming through.

11. Do not get involved in mortgages where the payments can be widely varied by elements outside your control, such as a sudden surge in interest rates. Do not take all your mortgages at a variable rate. At worst, have a 50/50 split between fixed-rate and variable-rate mortgages.

12. Do not get into properties which have substantial negative cashflows; that is, where your expenses substantially exceed your income.

And always remember: it is wise to live within your means and re-invest your profits. It is better to be inconspicuously wealthy, than to be ostentatiously poor.

Summary

Here's your checklist so far:

⇨ Be creative and flexible in your property dealings.

⇨ Make a plan based on your true net worth—and stick to it.

⇨ Look for properties with income and growth.

⇨ Master the 'dos and don'ts' of real estate.

In Chapter 9, we'll discuss the importance of property consultants—and why you need them.

Working with Property Consultants

Independent consultants are a growing force within commercial real estate. Indeed, many serious property investors now employ their own consultants; even as a beginner you may want to consider doing likewise.

The rise of the skilled consultant is partially a response to the property crash of the late 1980s and early 1990s, when many investors found that traditional real estate agents—who are, of course, acting for the seller of a property—sometimes lacked the expertise (not to mention the independence) to provide satisfactory advice. So these various consultants (in the fields of property, the law and taxation), who in the past may have been concerned mainly with valuations and pre-purchase due diligence, are now taking on myriad tasks, spanning the entire buying, holding and selling process.

They handle things such as:

- providing reports on the market, including the present status of the various sectors and the outlook for coming years

- finding properties that are appropriate for your specific investment strategy

- providing guidance on the fair price for properties in which you are interested

- devising a strategy for you to buy as cheaply as possible at auction

- conducting due diligence on each property you purchase

- advising on your finance options

- helping you with your taxation strategies

- management of your property (this is covered in Chapter 20)

- resolving any legal issues

- devising a creative marketing program for selling and leasing your property.

Establishing Your Team of Consultants

If you are a serious investor—and it's hard to imagine someone plunging into commercial real estate without being serious about it—it is important that you get your 'team' in place before you head out into the market. Then, when you do find your property, you don't have to waste valuable time interviewing and appointing these consultants. You should have at least already spoken to them by phone, and set up an initial rapport with them.

Commercial property transactions have a higher degree of complexity than do residential property transactions, so it is important that the professionals you are dealing with are familiar with all aspects of commercial property. Then, when a problem or dispute or novel situation arises, they can quickly come back to you, explain what has happened and give you recommendations as to how you should proceed.

Take the example of a conveyancer, who handles the paperwork in property deals. If something untoward arises, he or she will tell you what the problem is and ask how you wish to proceed. Their role is to process paper, not to give legal advice. For straightforward transactions that's fine; but not when complications arise.

There's an old saying: nothing's a problem until it's a problem, and then it costs you money.

Another example: you need to decide—in advance—in what vehicle you're going to buy the property. Will it be simply in your own name, or in the names of you and your spouse? Perhaps you wish to create a trust, or a company, or a partnership. (See Chapter 19 for more on these various alternatives.)

Each option has advantages and disadvantages. This is where a tax accountant can resolve a lot of the difficulties early on, rather than your going off and buying a property in your own name, and then later deciding you want to put it in a different structure.

Be aware that different professionals will have their specialties. If you are buying a multimillion dollar property complex you might not use the same lawyer as for the purchase of a property of less than a million dollars.

It's the same with accountants. You may want highly sophisticated tax advice, or estate planning advice, or some other kind of specialist service. In other words, it is important that your adviser be appropriate to your specific needs.

How do you Locate such Professionals?

Don't simply respond to attractive advertising.

The first step for many will be to find a competent property consultant. The chances are that he or she will be able to recommend an appropriate lawyer, accountant and finance broker.

Whether it is in the area of property, the law or taxation, ask around. Talk to people who have done some property investment—if a particular consultant has done a good job for them, this person is likely to do a good job for you. Also, thoroughly check out their websites—are they eager to give you loads of helpful information, or are the sites merely corporate brochures?

Do not be offended if it takes several phone calls to get through to the recommended consultant. The best consultants (whether property, legal or accounting) are not sitting in their offices— they're out putting deals together for their clients.

Finally, the key to success in creating a sound portfolio is to look at enough real estate to be able to recognise a good opportunity. Often you do not have enough time to do this yourself, so look through the eyes of a trusted property consultant. It will usually pay dividends.

[Summary]

Commercial property transactions have a higher degree of complexity than do residential property transactions. That's one reason many serious property investors now employ consultants. Even as a beginner you might consider doing likewise. A good consultant can save you precious money and time, and will know where to find the best properties.

The next chapter outlines your eight investment objectives.

Your Eight
Investment Objectives

chapter 10

Creating Your Own Blueprint

Okay, so you have worked through some 'global' issues to help crystallise your overall strategy. Now it is time to build your list of specific investment objectives and buying criteria, to help you acquire those properties within your preferred price range.

Since 1913, Gardner+Lang have had the chance to observe what some of the leading property investors (and their lenders) seem to adopt as the key elements for continued success. And though certain objectives and criteria might come and go with changing economic circumstances, we believe there are basically 20 key elements which have endured over the years.

These are the subject of this chapter and the next one. You might care to consider them as part of your planning process.

Eight Property Investment Objectives

In formulating your own investment strategy, you may choose to vary the specific order of importance for the following set of objectives. And it's up to you to determine exactly how they fit within your overall strategy. Furthermore, you are likely to have competing objectives. And, therefore, you will need to develop plans and policies to decide just how you'll achieve each of those separate objectives. Let's look at those key investment objectives that seem to have stood the test of time:

1. Enduring value.

2. Ongoing cashflow.

3. Steady growth.

4. Super growth.

5. Lending appeal.

6. Future collateral.

7. Cost control.

8. Tax benefits.

Enduring Value

Assuming you are a longer term investor (and not simply a short-term speculator) you've probably already discovered from this book that a property's enduring value—remaining attractive even after many years, and after several changes of tenant— relates to an understanding of market trends (both cyclical and emerging), how they will affect different types of property and in what timeframe. Therefore, enduring value needs to be at the top of your list of key objectives.

Ongoing Cashflow

A well-located investment, but with no assurance of ongoing income, will be of no help to you in meeting your ongoing mortgage payments. So, you always need to look well past the initial few years whenever you acquire your investment properties. And that's why it is so important to get your marketing strategy established, from the outset. This should ensure that you have several options down the track when it comes time to sell or re-lease the property.

Steady Growth

Although, in recent years, inflation has been under control, you still need to ensure that each investment will provide you with steady, predictable capital growth. Such properties will vary in type, depending upon specific location (Australia-wide) and a foreseeable market for that type of property at the time.

Super Growth

With a good consultant on your side, you'll occasionally come across investments which will provide you with a real opportunity for growth—above and beyond what the market will normally deliver. Sometimes this comes from a clever change of use. Sometimes it comes from subdividing a larger property into smaller components. So, always be alert for such gems to help you accelerate your portfolio's overall value. And, as you start to fully understand the impact of your buying criteria, you'll be better able to zero in on exactly which properties can deliver you this type of accelerated growth.

Lending Appeal

This includes all the vital elements—things like a secure cashflow, long leases, low maintenance requirements and a good location—that keep your financier happy. You need to start seeing each of your potential investments from a lender's point of view. That way, you'll know that almost every funding presentation you make will be successful.

Future Collateral

Being able to borrow money at the outset is vitally important. However, you also need to look a little further ahead—to when a certain portion of your core portfolio should be viewed as being held long term—to give comfort to your financiers, and to underpin your future capacity to borrow.

Cost Control

Even though your rental stream may be quite secure, wherever possible you should seek properties which have net leases (where your tenant pays all the building outgoings).

Why is this important? Because without skilful management, your operating costs for a given property (rates, taxes, maintenance, service contracts and so on) may suddenly start to escalate and unexpectedly affect your overall return.

For that reason, you need to protect yourself on two fronts. Being able to control your costs can improve your bottom line just as effectively as increasing your rentals.

Tax Benefits

Of your eight objectives, any likely tax benefits need to be viewed as a secondary—rather than as your principal—motive for making an acquisition.

There's no doubt that you can obtain significant benefits (and shelter your income) through depreciation allowances. But if the deal doesn't prove viable before potential tax benefits are taken into account, you ought not to be making the acquisition in the first place. See Chapter 19 for an extensive treatment of the tax benefits of commercial property.

Summary

Here they are again, your eight investment objectives:

1. Enduring value.

2. Ongoing cashflow.

3. Steady growth.

4. Super growth.

5. Lending appeal.

6. Future collateral.

7. Cost control.

8. Tax benefits.

In the next chapter we'll add to these your 12 individual buying criteria.

Your Twelve Buying Criteria

In order to satisfy the investment objectives that we discussed in the previous chapter, you will need to set certain buying criteria. It is against these that you can rate each and every property investment you undertake. These criteria are ranked in what has (over the years) become accepted by most investors as being their relative importance for making sound property investments.

Tenant Calibre and Lease Term

These two criteria alone could prove to be the most important for achieving your investment objectives. With a strong corporate (or government) tenant and a minimum of a five-year lease term, you are well on your way to making a successful investment.

Recent Construction and Flexible Design

Generally, whenever a property has been recently built, it will have ongoing appeal to subsequent tenants and require less renovation to maintain its modern appearance. This will help to ensure that many of your objectives are met.

It also means you'll start to enjoy significant tax benefits, thanks to generous depreciation allowances in a building's early life.

Likewise, a flexible design means that you are not left with an inefficient floor layout if your principal tenant were to vacate at the end of lease term. You will have an easily adaptable layout which will allow you to draw from a wide market when re-letting is required.

And at that point, you can enjoy further tax benefits from depreciating any of the refurbishment works that may be required.

Lease Structure and Absence of Competition

Lease structure relates to things like the frequency and method of your rent reviews, who pays the operating costs and to what degree a tenant is responsible for total building maintenance. All these elements are negotiated on a deal-by-deal basis, but will have a big impact upon many of your objectives.

Absence of competition relates to how many similar properties there are near yours, and is simply a matter of comparing various investment opportunities that you have—one against another. This determines whether the market could become over-saturated, which may affect your return from the property or cause difficulties when it comes to re-letting.

Good Position and Emerging Trends

All other things being equal, the better the location, the better your property will perform. Many factors—some of them subjective—determine what constitutes a good location. It depends on the nature of the property, and includes issues such as visibility, accessibility to public transport and position within an established area for that type of property. But, as with the other criteria, this one alone should not be your sole determinant.

What do we mean by emerging trends? Well, they can include demographic trends, such as population movements, which invariably lead to many new investment opportunities. But equally, new trends are emerging in relation to construction, design, energy conservation, security, lift technology, automation and so on. All of these will affect the future demand for, and appeal of, the properties in question.

Taking quick advantage of a new trend can dramatically improve the performance of any properties you may already own, not to mention giving you the ability to enhance underperforming properties you may be looking to acquire or develop.

Keep a keen eye out for hidden opportunities to (inexpensively) gain a competitive advantage.

Passing Yield and Zoning

Passing yield refers to the current yield for an existing investment. If it is derived from rentals that are considered to be 'above market'—that is, higher than the rents currently being paid by the tenants of similar properties—you are unlikely to receive any increases from your market reviews. Alternatively, if the rental is below market and your future reviews are fixed—

91

meaning that you cannot increase the rent 'to market', even if property values and rentals are soaring—or are incremental reviews or are tied to the Consumer Price Index, then you'll only be adding to (and deferring) your problem until the lease expires.

On the other hand, your passing yield may be at market rentals. This should mean you will be able to enjoy an improving cashflow, and maybe even some super growth if you have seen an opportunity which other investors may have overlooked.

Zoning relates to your property's present and potential future uses. This type of information is available from your local council.

Sometimes a property can have a Non-Conforming Use Permit, which could allow a residential property to be used as an office. While it can be used for offices now, it may only ever be able to be developed for residential purposes.

If (historically) there have been a large number of these types of non-conforming properties in a given locality, some inner-city municipalities have been introducing 'mixed use' zoning to legitimise (and actually encourage) the coexistence of such a rich diversity of uses. It's something you need to be on top of, as there are specific zoning and density changes occurring on a regular basis, and you can often make windfall gains if you are astute.

Title Options and Vendor Motivation

A property surveyor will be able to tell you (with little expense) if you are able to subdivide the title for a parcel of land or an entire building, in which case you are able to significantly enhance your property's marketability and, therefore, what it is worth.

You may still choose to sell the property as a whole, but new purchasers could be attracted to it because of the added flexibility of being able to sell off a portion of the property, should the need arise. And people pay a handsome premium for that flexibility, often well in excess of your cost of creating it.

Vendor motivation is important, but ought not be your principal reason for buying a specific property. Having assessed all the fundamentals, and satisfied your earlier criteria, a motivated vendor will invariably provide you with some additional interesting benefits. These can range from leaving some money in the property at a low rate, on second mortgage, to allowing you to upvalue (see below) all the plant and equipment, so that you can depreciate them from a much higher base.

Sometimes a vendor specifies the written-down value of the plant and equipment (that is, chattels) of a property. More often than not, though, the contract is 'silent' on the precise value of these items. This allows you to apportion the contract price by valuing the plant and equipment at their current-day value, thereby depreciating these items from a higher base and giving you a greater tax benefit. This is 'upvaluing'.

With a motivated vendor, your prime focus quickly moves away from the price and starts concentrating on how to structure the most attractive contract terms.

[Summary]

Here are the twelve individual buying criteria:

1. Tenant calibre.

2. Lease term.

3. Recent construction.

4. Flexible design.

5. Lease structure.

6. Absence of competition.

7. Good position.

8. Emerging trends.

9. Passing yield.

10. Zoning.

11. Title options.

12. Vendor motivation.

In the next chapter, we shall look again at the main sectors of commercial property—retail, industrial and office—to help you determine which is best for you.

Then, in Chapter 13, we shall merge the eight investment objectives and twelve buying criteria into a matrix, which you can use to rate every potential investment.

Having a Look at What's Out There

As you are aware from previous chapters, you need to be sure of your underlying aspirations and decide what exactly you want out of your investment. Be specific:

- ➲ Are you after a lucrative cashflow?

- ➲ Do you want a profitable overall yield?

- ➲ Do you need tax savings?

- ➲ Are you looking for a hedge against inflation?

Knowing precisely what you want will affect your choice of properties. It will also help you to structure the kind of deal which best serves your interests.

Do not be in a tearing hurry. There is a large range of properties for your consideration. Do not just settle for an investigation of, say, industrial properties in one favoured area. Such a limited vision denies you the full range of possibilities.

Take into account the current health of the wider financial world—the economy, interest rates, share prices and so on—and analyse how they affect prices of investment property. In the end, these things do have an impact on the general investment climate—although, over the long haul, real estate prices are not wildly volatile and their recovery, after times of downturn, is generally quite fast. Historically, real estate seems to come out on top.

Retail Sector

Shops and blocks of shops along 'strip centres' will generally provide you a profitable return on the capital outlay, as long as two important conditions are met:

1. They must be in a good location.

2. They must have a sound tenant mix.

Location is vital because it affects both the retail sales turnover (to which rents are related) and capital appreciation.

If, for instance, you decide to buy a single shop, look for a street where the local council is doing beautification work—putting paving on the footpaths instead of asphalt, erecting benches and seats, planting shrubs and flowers, and so on—to create an attractive environment. Then, if you see a chance to move in and buy a shop, renovate it and put in a good tenant, it could be your chance to make a good investment.

On the other hand, you should generally steer clear of a location where everyone is moving out because a new supermarket has opened somewhere else. (Mind you, if you can pick up a group of three or four shops cheaply because the area is declining, you can create a professional service centre with, for example, an accountant, a firm of lawyers and a vet. These types of businesses do not rely so heavily on passing shoppers. Real estate always provides openings for lateral thinkers.)

The tenant mix is important, because there must be a sufficient variety of retailers to attract good shopper traffic, and not too many retailers in such direct competition that they damage each other's viability.

Beware of too many parasites—banks, building societies, travel agents and (yes) real estate agents—who move into a location simply because the retailers are creating excitement and attracting shoppers. They tend to live off that shopper traffic; that is, they take advantage of the success of a particular shopping centre, without bringing in many

A major supermarket chain can be a good retail tenant.

additional shoppers themselves. They also create 'dead spots'— if you have a shop in the middle of a group of these businesses you may find that fewer potential customers pass by—and they can push up rents beyond the reach of the traditional retailers.

Selecting a shop for investment also requires you to look into parking facilities and the weight of pedestrian traffic enjoying the benefits of retail competition. A good rule of thumb: always try to get in the middle of where the action is.

Industrial Sector

The growth of small service businesses over recent years has boosted the demand for small factories and showrooms, particularly in areas close to major regional centres.

Provided sufficient care is taken to select a good tenant, industrial property could suit the passive investor.

Factories need relatively low maintenance and have low outgoing costs and, provided sufficient care is taken to select a good tenant, could well suit the passive investor.

A point to note: investors going into small industrial properties should make sure, wherever possible, there is sufficient room available for expansion as the tenants' businesses grow—you don't want to constrain the growth of successful tenants due to space limitations. It is better to have spare space at the start than have a tenant operating in cramped conditions, just waiting for the lease to expire in order to relocate to larger premises.

Office Sector

Office accommodation is particularly appealing, because it allows for the full spectrum of investors —from those putting money into single shop-front offices to those developing multistorey city complexes.

Offices are appealing because they allow for the full spectrum of investors.

One exciting recent development is the opening up of a whole new field of smaller strata-titled offices, offering smaller investors an entry price as low as $100,000, with a net yield of between 6.00 and 6.25 per cent per annum, and with funding for up to 70 per cent of the value.

A Useful Tip...

In the early days of property portfolio building, in order to efficiently manage your property, do not roam too far away. Stay within your 'buying radius'—and that means roughly within 15 to 20 minutes from your home or office. This will mean that you are investing in an area you are familiar with, and will allow you to keep a closer eye on your investment. This can be helpful for the beginner. There will still be a large range of investments to choose from.

Stick to nearby properties until you have a fairly large portfolio and therefore more experience, at which point you may benefit from using a professional property manager or feel more comfortable investing further away.

Summary

It is important to work out your objectives before you buy, then examine the main investment sectors— retail, industrial and office—to find the most appropriate investment.

In the next chapter we shall take the eight investment objectives from Chapter 10 and the twelve buying criteria from Chapter 11, and merge them into a simple matrix to make it easy for you to rate every potential investment that you might consider.

How to Rate Property Investment Opportunities

[chapter 13]

Making the Task Really Easy

You have already covered quite a lot of the material needed to help you achieve your investment objectives. But, while you may have found it interesting (and even helpful), you may now be wondering how you can put it into practice.

At this point, you might even be thinking that it all seems rather confusing—perhaps even a little disjointed—and, most likely, something you could only fully master with a fair amount of training, plus several years of practical experience.

If only there was a way—you may be thinking—that you could condense all this guidance into a simple checklist, to give you an easy-to-use method of rating each property you are about to consider.

Put all your concerns to rest. We have just such a matrix for you. Below is the Gardner+Lang Property Rating Matrix, shown here as it appears on their website.

Figure 13.1: **The Property Rating Matrix**

YOUR BUYING CRITERIA	How well these buying criteria meet ... YOUR INVESTMENT OBJECTIVES							
	Enduring Value	Ongoing Cash flow	Steady Growth	Super Growth	Lending Appeal	Future Collateral	Cost Control	Depr'n Benefits
Tenant Calibre	✓	✓	✓	✓	✓	✓	✓	
Lease Term	✓	✓	✓	✓	✓	✓	✓	
Recent Construction	✓	✓	✓		✓	✓	✓	✓
Flexible Design	✓	✓	✓	✓		✓	✓	✓
Lease Structure	✓	✓	✓	✓	✓	✓	✓	
Absence of Competition	✓	✓	✓	✓	✓	✓		
Good Position	✓	✓	✓	✓	✓	✓		
Emerging Trends	✓	✓	✓	✓	✓	✓		
Passing Yield	✓	✓		✓	✓	✓		
Zoning	✓			✓	✓	✓		
Title Options	✓			✓		✓		
Vendor Motivation		✓		✓				✓

How Does it Work?

The boxes with a tick indicate where each of your buying criteria (from Chapter 11) will help to meet a specific investment objective (from Chapter 10). The final rating you give for each criteria is simply your assessment of how well this specific buying criteria (in the left-hand column) is actually being met by each property.

Note that the various buying criteria have been ranked to reflect what is generally accepted as their relative importance. As you read across the lines for each of the various criteria, you will quickly identify the respective investment objectives each criteria is seeking to fulfil. The shaded areas are where specific criteria make no significant contribution to meeting your objectives.

Different weightings (from 15 to 3) have been given to each criteria to reflect their relative importance. These are used to arrive at a final, overall score. These weightings are based on the many years of experience of Gardner+Lang. You can take advantage of this matrix at the company's website (www.gal.com.au/rsl/matrix). Once you have gained extensive experience yourself in commercial property, you should be able to devise your own—personalised—system of weightings.

As you start to assess each potential investment, what you need to do is rate how well each of your various buying criteria (and, therefore, your specific investment objectives) is met. With very little practice, you'll soon be able to *quantify* what would otherwise be a *subjective* assessment.

If a criteria was to record a 'perfect' score, it would receive a rating of 10. And, if it falls short in any way, the rating would obviously be reduced—where zero would mean the property failed to meet that specific buying criteria in any way.

Your actual level of experience is not all that vital—so long as it is *you* who rates each buying criteria for the chosen property. That way, there is a consistency for the ratings because they are each viewed through the 'same set of eyes'.

Here's an Example

So far, we have covered the theory and logic behind this quick and simple method of rating a bundle of properties to help you create a short-list for serious further analysis. Let's now run through an example of how this would work. In order to make it more meaningful, you'll need to visualise a hypothetical, two-level suburban office building, worth about $850,000.

From here, you simply complete the table below by filling in your ratings in the final column, and you're able to quickly compute a property rating.

Figure 13.2: The Property Rating Matrix – Example

YOUR BUYING CRITERIA	How well these Buying Criteria meet ... YOUR INVESTMENT OBJECTIVES								RATING 1 – 10
	Enduring Value	Ongoing Cash flow	Steady Growth	Super Growth	Lending Appeal	Future Collateral	Cost Control	Depr'n Benefits	
Tenant Calibre	✓	✓	✓	✓	✓	✓	✓		7
Lease Term	✓	✓	✓	✓	✓	✓	✓		8
Recent Construction	✓	✓	✓		✓	✓	✓	✓	8
Flexible Design	✓	✓	✓	✓		✓	✓	✓	6
Lease Structure	✓	✓	✓	✓	✓	✓	✓		8
Absence of Competition	✓	✓	✓	✓	✓	✓			5
Good Position	✓	✓	✓	✓	✓	✓			8
Emerging Trends	✓	✓	✓	✓	✓	✓			8
Passing Yield	✓	✓		✓	✓	✓			9
Zoning	✓			✓	✓	✓			9
Title Options	✓			✓		✓			9
Vendor Motivation		✓		✓				✓	3

The overall score for this property is 74%.

On the following page you will see how these ratings were arrived at.

BUYING CRITERIA	YOUR ASSESSMENT	YOUR RATING
Tenant Calibre	A corporate tenant, with directors' guarantees	**7**
Lease Term	Five years remaining on the present lease	**8**
Recent Construction	About three years old	**8**
Flexible Design	The floor layout and services do not allow for leasing into smaller tenancies	**6**
Lease Structure	There are three-yearly market reviews at the landlord's option, with 5 per cent per annum fixed increases in between	**8**
Absence of Competition	The property is located in an area with a number of other similar office buildings	**5**
Good Position	On a main arterial road, with easy parking and close to good public transport	**8**
Emerging Trends	The building contains modern data cabling, and already has optical fibre installed	**8**
Passing Yield	The rental is (if anything) a little below market	**9**
Zoning	The property is in an appropriate office zoning	**9**
Title Options	The location of the entry foyer allows for division of the building, to create a separate title for each of the floors	**9**
Vendor Motivation	Unfortunately, the vendor has no borrowings on the property, and is happy to wait until the property's market value is achieved	**3**

Everyone will have their own idea of what is an acceptable overall score. However, our view is that you should generally look to have your property scoring 70 per cent or better, before you consider further investigation of a potential acquisition.

You'll notice that simply adding the individual ratings we gave to each criteria provides a total of 88—this is because not all criteria carry exactly the same weighting.

Where Do You Go From There?

Well, from there, you would move to the more detailed feasibility stage—looking at projected cashflows over at least a 4-year (and sometimes up to a 10-year) period. This involves calculating an internal rate of return, to more closely compare the properties on your short-list.

An interactive version of the Property Rating Matrix is available online, where you can simply enter your ratings for each property and have that property rating immediately calculated for you. Just go to www.gal.com.au/rsl/matrix.

Summary

You'll find the Property Rating Matrix a valuable tool for judging whether a particular investment opportunity is really appropriate for your needs. The more you use it, the more familiar with it you will become.

Now let's take a look at what you need to know about financing your property.

Borrowing for a Greater Profit

One of the attractions of commercial property is the manner in which it is possible to leverage your equity through borrowing. And in that way, you can considerably enhance the return on your equity. In fact, if the loan is structured correctly (that is, your net income from the property exceeds your interest repayments), you can enjoy a positive cashflow right from the time you take possession of your investment, thanks to the high yields of commercial property and relatively low interest rates.

Contrast that with borrowing to buy shares or residential property—where, nowadays, it is extremely difficult to maintain a positive cashflow while still meeting your interest payments. This is due to the comparatively low yields on these investments, and the lack of any special taxation benefits, such as generous depreciation allowances (see Chapter 19 for more detail on taxation and depreciation).

Putting Your Finance to Work

Here is an actual example of projected after-tax cashflow for the first four years of a newly built Melbourne office investment property, returning an initial net yield of 6.25 per cent per annum.

The total acquisition cost is $265,000 (which includes items like property consultant fees, legal costs and stamp duty). As the buyer, you would be contributing $87,000, and your borrowings the remaining $178,000. In this example, your tax is at a rate of 30 per cent.

Based on a 3+3 year lease (three years, plus an option for a further three years), the rent would rise by 3 per cent each year for the first three years. Then, at the end of this period (and on exercise of the option to continue with the lease) a review based on market conditions would set a higher new rental for the fourth year, with subsequent annual rises of 3 per cent. (In this example, the rental increase at the end of the initial three-year term is based on our forecasts for the office property market—see Chapter 5.) The figures are shown opposite.

At the end of a four-year period, the property should attain a price of some $365,000. Were you to sell it and repay your loan, then (based on your initial equity of $87,000) the overall after-tax return you have received calculates out at more than 19 per cent per annum—which is after selling costs and paying capital gains tax.

You are able to achieve these sorts of after-tax returns by borrowing, and using less of your own money.

Risks

Sudden rises in interest rates could of course send the above calculations askew, and some investors therefore choose to lock-in their major expense—interest payments—using a fixed-rate loan. However, unless you have expertise in this area yourself, this is a matter that should be determined in conjunction with your finance broker.

Table 14.1: **After-Tax Cashflow – Example**

COMPONENT	YEAR 1	YEAR 2	YEAR 3	YEAR 4
(a) Net rental (after management fee)	$14,538	$14,974	$15,423	$19,279
(b) *less* Interest per annum (at 7.4%)	$13,172	$13,172	$13,172	$13,172
(c) Cashflow before tax (a) minus (b)	$1,366	$1,802	$2,251	$6,107
(d) *less* Depreciation allowance	$10,727	$9,380	$8,020	$6,989
(e) Taxable income (c) minus (d)	($9,361)	($7,578)	($5,769)	($882)
(f) Tax rebate 30% of (e)	$2,808	$2,273	$1,731	$265
Total after-tax cashflow (c) plus (f)	**$4,174**	**$4,075**	**$3,982**	**$6,372**

The other main risk is that circumstances like an economic downturn (or office market oversupply) could mean you lose your tenant and struggle to find a new one. This would also have some impact on the value of the property.

Some Frequently Asked Questions

How do you apply for a loan?

Talk to your bank. Every bank has a range of commercial loan products. However the best results are often achieved using the services of a finance broker.

What information do you need?

The lender will require full details of the property—including an independent valuation (it may even insist on arranging its own valuation)—along with sufficient information that gives them the confidence that you are able to repay the loan.

What interest rates should you expect to pay?

Commercial property loans generally carry interest rates a little higher than those for residential property.

What fees might be involved?

Fees can vary widely, and can involve all kinds of factors, including your relationship with the lender and the prevailing level of competition between lenders.

How long does a loan go for?

Each lender has different products, including fixed-period loans and interest-only loans that might extend indefinitely. Much depends on your own circumstances and requirements.

What deposit is necessary?

When buying commercial property the banks will not generally lend more than about 60 to 70 per cent of the value of the property, so you will be responsible for the remainder.

Are loans for commercial property hard to get?

Banks tend to judge an application for a loan for commercial property using the same risk criteria as they would for lending for any other purpose.

Finding a Lender

Most major financial institutions—including banks, insurance companies, building societies, co-operatives, specialist financial lenders, friendly societies and others—have developed products for investors in commercial property. Some solicitors can also arrange finance.

This is an ever-changing area. Competition and the growing sophistication of investors have led to a range of innovative new products and schemes, such as revolving credit facilities, whereby investors can borrow unspecified amounts—up to a particular limit—to meet their changing requirements, with flexible repayment schedules. Many institutions have details on their websites.

Commercial property can be a complex field—much more so than residential property—and so we recommend that you expand your education by visiting these sites. Read as much as you can. And make sure you use the various calculators.

Nevertheless, when it actually comes time to borrow, we would suggest that you employ the services of a finance broker.

Why? Because when looking to finance a commercial property acquisition, it is vital that you understand certain key points about how the money market really works. Otherwise, you could find yourself borrowing at an unfavourable rate that could have a detrimental impact on the return on your investment.

All major lending institutions operate within certain parameters of risk. One way of mitigating risk is to maintain a spread of loans across many sectors. Thus, the institutions will seek to achieve a balance between, say, commercial and residential property lending. And even within commercial property, they will work to maintain a balance between the various sectors.

So the crucial point to understand is that at any point in time, a particular financial institution (based on its current loan book) might need to balance its new lending in particular areas of the market. This is to avoid overexposure (or underexposure) to any one sector.

As a result, there are times when one institution might temporarily be offering preferential rates for mortgages for particular kinds of property, in order to boost its exposure to that sector.

Conversely, at the same time, another institution might be working to reduce its exposure to that area of the market, through various penalties, including higher interest rates.

For example, an institution might temporarily add, say, an additional three-quarters of a percentage point to its rate for particular properties, which compensates itself for the risk of being overexposed.

As we mentioned in a previous chapter, you might be a seasoned investor with two or three institutions that have historically 'looked after' you; that doesn't mean that at any given point they are the best for you (though the prospect of losing all your existing business with an institution may be sufficient to force it to drop its rates for a new loan).

The simple fact is that, unless property investment is your full-time business, and you are prepared to spend the time to physically go around and visit and negotiate with all the many institutions, you are generally better off using a finance broker.

Working with a Finance Broker

Finance brokers receive regular updates from myriad financial institutions, some of them probably unknown to most investors.

On a daily basis, they generally know where to find the cheapest money for your particular investment. Thus, once they know your particular requirements and your asset situation, they won't even waste your time by trying certain institutions; they may instead head straight for a lender that would never have been your first port of call—indeed, one you might not even have heard of.

The broker understands the manner in which the application needs to be presented, and will likely complete most of the paperwork for you. He or she knows which are the particularly relevant parts of a lender's documents. By contrast, if you are dealing directly with a bank or some other institution, you need to handle the volume of documentation yourself.

A broker can sometimes even get a better rate for you at your own bank, thanks to specialist knowledge of current rates, and being able to 'threaten' your bank—ever so subtly.

[Summary]

Through the leverage of borrowing money, it is possible to greatly magnify your property holdings and your after-tax investment returns. And when it comes to borrowing, it is usually better to use the services of a professional finance broker, who can likely save you a considerable amount of money.

With your finance in place, let's now examine the key topic of negotiation.

Being Able
to Clinch the Deal

If you are looking to buy property privately, you must face the fact that there will be one-to-one negotiations. Therefore, you need to have some knowledge—and preferably some expertise —of how to negotiate. (See also Appendix C, 'How to Negotiate Your Way to Success'.)

Let's look at how different people see negotiations:

> Everything is negotiable. Almost daily we see intractable positions change as a result of effective negotiating and exchange of concessions. In most cases they come to form win/win situations, where both parties are able to go to their separate supporters and claim acceptable success 'in exchange for a few minor concessions'.
>
> —*Peter Middleton, General Manager of John P. Young & Associates (SA) Pty Ltd*

> One of the most formidable weapons of professional negotiators is silence. Most people hate silence and will attempt to fill it with information—which is exactly what you want. Train yourself to say in every one of your negotiations: 'If everything goes wrong, will my life end?'

—*Herbert A. Cohen, professional negotiator, author of* You Can Negotiate Anything

> Let us begin anew—remembering on both sides that civility is not a sign of weakness, and sincerity is always subject to proof. Let us never negotiate out of fear. But let us never fear to negotiate.

—*John F. Kennedy*

> Negotiation is getting what you want.

—*Robert J. Laser, business consultant*

As you're probably now aware, there are three key elements in negotiations:

1. Information.
2. Time.
3. Power.

Getting the Information

Someone said that 'to be forewarned is to be forearmed', and information is your forewarning. Find out everything you can about the property you want to buy, and especially about the person or firm from whom you want to buy it, and about their agent.

Most investors assume that the various items on their 'agenda' in a negotiation are the same as the vendor's. But in all my (Chris's) years of acting for investors, I can't recall when both parties ever had identical issues that were held to be vital for a successful outcome.

Scott M. Smith, a major property player among the sun-seeker set at Fort Lauderdale in Florida, spells out some of the things you need to know about the vendor:

➲ Why is he selling?

➲ Does he have family or personal commitments?

➲ Is he moving interstate or overseas?

➲ Does he have other settlements falling due?

➲ Does he have a cash problem or a cashflow problem?

➲ Is he being forced to sell for some other reason?

Smith says:

> You have to ask these questions in the course of conversation. By being genuinely interested in the sellers as people, you can make them (or their agent) feel comfortable giving you much of this information. With a little practice you'll find that it's not hard to ask a lot of questions and get straight answers.

Herb Cohen wrote in *You Can Negotiate Anything*:

> What you want to know going into the negotiation process are the real limits on the other side ... the extent beyond which they will not go.

Time Will Change Things

Cohen wrote further:

> Don't be surprised when you receive the initial rejection to your proposal. 'No' is a reaction not a position. With the passage of sufficient time and repeated effort on your part every 'no' can be transformed into a 'maybe' and, perhaps, eventually a 'yes'.

Sometimes an excellent deal can be done by grasping an unexpected chance quickly. If you have fast access to money you can snatch a property that comes on the market without warning, offered by a vendor who urgently needs to sell, often at a reduced price.

But that is the exception. In most negotiations it is a plus to possess a great deal of patience. The fact is that deadlines are often fictitious, products themselves of the negotiating process: 'Let's get this deal wrapped up by Friday.' Generally, they are usually more flexible than you realise.

Shifts in position are made predominantly towards the end of a negotiation, not at the beginning when the parties are trying to get the feel of a deal. It has long been established in negotiations that 80 per cent of the concessions are made in the last 20 per cent of time allocated to them—an important fact according to Roger Dawson, author of *You Can Get Anything You Want – But You Have to Do More Than Ask*. This means that if you know when the other person's negotiating deadline is, you know when most of the concessions are going to come.

Find out their deadline—you could be better off if you don't make concessions or really try to consummate the deal until you are into that last 20 per cent of time available.

Perceptions of Power

Herb Cohen likes to tell the following to his seminars round the world (although he might just be quoting the great car maker Henry Ford):

> Power is based on perception. If you think you've got it, then you've got it. If you think you don't have it (even if you've got it), then you don't have it.

Power in itself is neither good nor bad. It is simply a vehicle for moving somebody from one point of view to another. So let's look at some of the sources of power.

Power of Competition

This happens when you can legitimately create the perception of having options. When I (Chris) talk to first-time investors, I explain that they actually have considerable power when seeking a loan from their bank. They often say: 'You've got to be joking. They've got the money, so how do we have any power?'

It's simple—you're talking to one bank and you say to your partner who banks with another: 'Look, I'm not sure whether we should get the loan here, or perhaps from your bank?' More often than not they won't simply let you walk out the door.

Power of Legitimacy

This relates to the power of the 'printed word'.

If you think about it, our lives are ruled by written messages: 'Keep off the grass', 'Wet paint' (mind you in Australia we seem to be somewhat cynical—we want to touch it first to check), 'No cash refunds', and so on.

Salespeople quickly learn the power of the printed word. Most contracts are typeset documents to which they add personal information by hand. They do this by asking reflex questions such as: 'What is your correct full name?'—questions to which people generally know the answer.

Once complete, the contract is given to the buyer to check the handwritten additions. And most buyers tend not to read the printed conditions in any detail, because they assume (wrongly) that they are non-negotiable. All 'standard' contracts evolve by negotiation over time. As such, they are negotiable, and should be challenged if they are inconsistent with the agreement you have finally reached.

Power of Involvement

The more time and money you can have somebody invest into a negotiation, the greater the chance you have of this person coming around to your point of view. It is therefore often better not to conclude the deal at your first meeting, even if that is possible. Find a reason to at least defer the need for a decision until the next time that you agree to meet. Otherwise, one party may feel they paid too much, while the other feels they should have asked for more.

Often it's useful to ask the other party how they would like to structure the deal. Surprisingly, you might find that you can live with much of what they will propose. So when you frame your offer (in their format), the other party will find it difficult to reject what they themselves have helped to create.

Power of Morality

When I first started in sales, I was told that there are only about seven or eight mean, nasty people in the world. Apparently, they move around a lot! But, basically, people are open and trustworthy. So, how can you use this in a 'high-powered' negotiation?

There comes a time in some negotiations when, to achieve any result at all, you have to place yourself at the mercy of the other party. You've reached an impasse, and all else seems to have failed. At such a time, you need to genuinely lower your guard and say to the other party: 'I need your help if we're going to put this deal together.' You will generally find that such a gesture will cause a similar move by them to open up and co-operate by suggesting ways in which the apparent gap in the negotiations may be bridged.

Believe me, it works—so long as your motives are completely genuine.

Power of Persistence

Sometimes persistence is all you have going for you.

We've already discussed how time can affect a negotiation, and the power of involvement. But persistence is taking it one step further. Just hanging in there when others have given up. We're not talking about simply 'flogging a dead horse'. Rather, it is a question of persevering when you have a clear belief that success will come, given time. And people enjoy doing business with somebody who shows a commitment to what they believe in, and a strong desire to bring it about.

The main thing to remember is that negotiation is a process, not an event. However, you need to make sure that you engage in the right process. And Robert Laser lays this out rather well in the table below.

Table 15.1: **Negotiating Tools and Outcomes**

PROCESS	RELATIONSHIP	RESULT
Persuasion	I Win – You Lose	Unsuccessful
Accommodation	I Lose – You Win	Unsuccessful
Compromise	I Lose – You Lose	Unsuccessful
Partnering	I Win – You Win	Successful

Expertise

Finally, expertise is another important negotiating tool. The other party tends to respect you if you clearly know what you are talking about. For this reason alone (although there are many others) it is wise for both the amateur or experienced property investor to take on the mantle of professionalism.

And, hopefully, what is included in Appendix B will provide you with the tools you'll need.

Summary

Mastering the tools of negotiation can mean the difference between success and failure. Much has been written on this topic, and we suggest you read widely.

Always remember to have as much information as possible at your disposal when you enter into negotiations. And be prepared to take your time. Often the most concessions are made towards the very end.

In Chapter 16 we want to explore some valuable examples of how to use your imagination in looking at investment opportunities.

Using Your Imagination

[chapter 16]

It's been a few years now, but here are two excellent examples of how, using your imagination, you can leverage big returns from an underperforming property. If you are in Victoria you can even visit them and judge for yourself. They come from co-author Chris Lang. One is an arcade, the other a shopping centre.

The Walk

The AMP Society held an architectural competition to arrive at several schemes for the replacement of five or six buildings fronting the Bourke Street mall opposite Melbourne's famous Myer and David Jones department stores. It was to be a $29 million development. However, because of union activity the Society was persuaded to look at holding, instead of developing.

AMP came to Gardner+Lang and asked us what we thought. Well, the annual yield for the proposed development was going to be about 3.8 per cent and we thought this return was too low as an investment. We saw ways of getting it up to around 4.2 per cent, but concluded that this was still not acceptable. So we thought some more about it, and suggested to the Society that they keep the buildings—rather than pull them down—and put an arcade through the middle of them.

We certainly did not get a lot of support from their architect, who could see a million-dollar fee flying out the window, because the cost was going to be much smaller than anticipated —around $2.5 million to $3.0 million.

Here is what happened:

Most of the upstairs areas were blocked off, as fire regulations made their renovation uneconomic. The arcade was pushed through, and we leased the ground floor and basement as trading floors, to Just Jeans and Dunklings, while Portmans took space in the basement, ground and first floors. The resulting yield was lifted to around 14 to 15 per cent—about three times better than the original plan—with a creative solution involving some 40 additional shops.

Generally, I am not wedded to keeping old buildings, but if you can make them work better than a new building—at a much lower capital cost—you should give it a shot.

Geelong Market Square

In company with two other agencies, Gardner+Lang were invited to tender to lease and manage the Geelong Market Square shopping centre in the heart of Geelong.

The brief was simple: to ensure, on behalf of Geelong City Council and the ratepayers, the most viable tenant mix, while also ensuring that traders in the centre could operate in an environment where they could achieve their maximum potential.

We were shown the plans before any site work was started, which is the way we prefer to work. At once, we could see a serious problem. Because of the limited size of the mid-city site, there would not be enough space to accommodate all the necessary major traders on the ground floor. Some would move to the first floor, and thus be deprived of people traffic. Additionally, about five ground-floor entrances were planned and this tended to fragment people traffic past each tenant's shop.

At that early stage, a basement car park was drawn in, so we suggested that an escalator take shoppers from the basement directly up to the first floor, bypassing the ground floor. This would give the shoppers a very good visual feel of what was in the whole centre, and they would walk back down to the supermarket on the ground floor. However, cost later ruled out a basement car park.

So we then suggested: 'Why not take the car park out of the basement, and put it on the first and second floors, with the entrance to shops on the first floor?' At the same time, we suggested the number of ground-floor pedestrian entrances be reduced. That was agreed.

As work went ahead, we started selecting tenants, giving particular consideration to the traders who were on the site beforehand, and preference at all times to viable local retailers. The result was that the centre was almost totally leased by the time it opened; today they need traffic lights in the elevated car park to control the 3,500 to 4,000 cars a day, which shuttle in and out of the 650 parking spots.

The two major tenants on the first floor found they did excellent business. The car park switch was an Australian first, and it worked.

[Summary]

A final checklist:

⇨   Always look to 'add value'.

⇨   Find new solutions to old problems.

⇨   If it pays, refurbish.

⇨   Think bold!

The Why, When and How of Selling Property

The popular perception is that commercial property ought to be viewed as a longer term investment—one that provides you with a stable and secure income, plus steady capital growth. Yet people's needs evolve and change over time. What was once an attractive investment may, for all kinds of reasons, become less appealing several years down the track. As a result, you may decide there is a need to sell.

For example, you may urgently need some (or all) of the money you've invested. Or perhaps you simply receive an offer that is too good to refuse. Or, you may believe that property prices are about to slump, and that you should get out while you are ahead.

But there are other less obvious reasons for selling as well, and the astute investor should be aware of these:

1. When you buy a property—even if it's not new—you are allowed under taxation legislation to 'upvalue' (raise the apportioned value) of plant and equipment, providing the contract does not specify a particular written-down value for these components. This can give you extremely valuable depreciation benefits for the early years of ownership.

   Plant and equipment (such as carpets, cabling, light fittings, lifts, heating and air conditioning) are usually depreciated on an accelerated basis. That is, depreciation is highest in the early years of your ownership. In fact, after five or six years, most of that type of depreciation has been claimed. (You'll find Chapter 19 gives you considerably more detail on taxation and depreciation.)

   When buying the property, the contract should not specify a value for the plant and equipment, as this would prevent you from upvaluing those highly depreciable components. But when you come to sell, it is equally important that you include their written-down value in the contract. Otherwise, you could well incur a balancing charge from the Tax Office, should the new owner decide to upvalue the plant and equipment again.

   As such, this could be your trigger point to sell, especially if you have just renewed a five-year lease contract on better terms, thus boosting the value of the property.

2. You might find that an older property (which you own) requires a major structural or capital upgrade. For example, the roof might need replacing. If you don't

have the ready cash it might be better to sell the property and pass these costs to the new owner.

3. You could own a property in an area where there are mooted zoning or road network changes. If there is less than, say, two years remaining on the lease, it might be possible to sell the property to a potential owner–occupier who is eager to take advantage of the 'blue sky' potential of the changes.

In fact, the mooted changes may not actually occur. But for as long as they appear a possibility, they could well make your property extremely appealing to certain prospective purchasers, offering you the chance of a substantial capital gain from its sale.

Successfully Marketing Your Property

Anyone who has sold a house will know that in the competitive world of real estate each of the many agents you talk to will claim to offer the best sales strategy. In fact, there is no definitive strategy. So what follows is a marketing program which has been proven successful many times by co-author Chris Lang and his firm Gardner+Lang. It is a strategy that has been formulated to help ensure the best possible outcome, through creatively targeting investors, developers and potential owner–occupiers, and by adopting a broad, yet cost-effective, marketing campaign, in order to draw out those buyers best suited to your property.

Choosing Your Method of Sale

The secret to successfully selling any property is to give your prospective buyers the feeling they could miss out. However, that is very hard to achieve with simply a straight, private sale. In fact, it might take longer to achieve a result with a private sale, as it fails to create any sense of urgency in a buyer's mind.

A further factor is that you are at a disadvantage in having to nominate an 'asking price'. Traditionally, you need to inflate this figure—to allow for the expected level of negotiation.

That can become a 'two-edged sword'. You could effectively deter potential buyers, because the figure is too far above their initial expectations. Or, it could go the other way: you may end up selling at a figure below what buyers may have been prepared to pay, had they been put under the pressure of competitive bidding.

Thus, a well-promoted public auction is often the most appropriate method of sale. That way, prospective buyers are all heading towards a fixed end-date, and there is no need for you to publicly nominate an actual selling price, so that you can maintain control all the way through.

An Innovative, Results-Driven Advertising Strategy

As you'll appreciate, media advertising can be very costly. And there is also a limit on just how much you can actually say about a property in any one advertisement. So, Gardner+Lang's approach is to *link* the media ads with dedicated internet pages, for each property we sell or lease. And this has proven to be very successful.

You will find most agents simply choose to place their properties onto the internet in a rather generic form, using portal sites such as property.com.au, realcommercial.com.au or propertylook.com.au. As such, a problem can arise in that every buyer actually looking for those properties needs to go through a lengthy search process, on one or more of the above websites. But what's even worse for you as a vendor, is that in the process of doing so, these buyers may well discover several other properties they prefer instead!

So, what we find works best is to create several dedicated web pages for your property on our website, and promote that specific web address in the media ads, the brochure and board. That means, prospective buyers can then *laser-in* on your property, to view and download much more information about it.

By using dedicated web pages, you are able to provide a detailed description of the property (over a number of pages), give details of the location and spell-out the benefits involved. You can also include photographs of the exterior and the internal layout.

Normally, you would be asked to spend about 1.5 per cent of the expected selling price on marketing your property. But, by adopting our creative, linked approach we have found that sellers can well achieve an even better result with considerable savings. All in all, it is proving to be a far more effective (and much cheaper) way for sellers to promote their properties.

What Else Can You Expect from Your Agent?

Your agent should be able to explain in some detail the current state of the market, as well as providing estimates of a likely price for the property. But there is lots more. By way of a checklist for you, a good agent should also:

1. Gather and collate all necessary information to ensure purchasers will be fully informed, and capable of making a decision to buy.

2. Liaise with you and your lawyers, to make sure the documentation is fully completed and correct.

3. Mail out brochures and letters (or more likely, send out personal emails) to those potential purchasers known to be currently active in the market.

4. Try to secure editorial coverage within the various media being used.

5. Qualify all the enquiries that are generated throughout the marketing campaign.

6. Arrange for the various inspections to take place.

7. Prepare prospective buyers for the actual auction itself.

8. Keep you advised as to progress, on at least a weekly basis.

9. Ensure all preparations are made, so that everything runs smoothly on the day of the auction.

10. Conduct the auction, and attend to the signing of the contracts with the successful purchasers.

11. Seek to ensure Section 27s (the form that allows for a release of your deposit 28 days after the contract is executed) are acknowledged, so that you can have an early release of the deposit.

12. Follow up with your lawyers to ensure that the documents have been executed to their satisfaction.

13. With the Section 27s in place, account to you with the deposit monies, 30 days after the auction, setting everything out in a detailed statement for the sale.

Fees

Agents typically charge 2.5 to 3.0 per cent (plus GST) of the actual price that appears on the contract, upon successfully selling the property. However, a flat-fee arrangement like this is not necessarily in your best interests. Gardner+Lang, like some other agents, often offers clients the option of incentive-based fees—where the percentage charged rises according to the price achieved for the property. The agent thus has a big incentive to aim for the highest price possible.

A typical, incentive-based fee scale that might be proposed for a property expected to sell in the $840,000 to $860,000 range might be as shown below.

Table 17.1: Incentive-based Fee Scale

PROPOSED RATE	APPLICABLE PRICE RANGE	CALCULATING THE OVERALL FEE		
		PROGRESSIVE	TOTAL	ACTUAL %
1%	Up to $450,000	$4,500	$4,500	1.00
2%	$450,001 to $650,000	$4,000	$8,500	1.31
5%	$650,001 to $850,000	$10,000	$18,500	2.18
10%	Over $850,000			

Hopefully this gives you some insight as to how to successfully market your commercial property, when the need arises. If you would like to look at a case study on how the overall marketing strategy comes together, you can simply go to: www.gal.com.au/new_award.html.

[Summary]

Commercial property is generally viewed as a long-term investment. But for a variety of reasons you may choose to sell.

A skilled agent is crucial for the successful marketing of your property. Make sure that your sales agent has a detailed knowledge of the market and is experienced in the most up-to-date marketing techniques.

Maybe you can't afford to buy a shopping centre or office building by yourself, but you can certainly step into the 'big league' by joining a private property syndicate. The next chapter explains how you can set about doing this.

Private
Property Syndicates

You've probably noticed that syndicated property ownership is booming. But why is that so?

Simply because, properly structured, a syndicate allows a smaller investor—someone with, say, $250,000 or less—to take advantage of a greatly enhanced range of attractive opportunities that might present themselves in the property market. At the same time, the risk is spread among a group of fellow investors, who also enjoy the security of professional management.

Syndicates differ from listed property trusts—to date, the favoured route for most smaller property investors—where your money becomes part of a very large pool that is invested in many properties, and where the performance is often more related to the sharemarket than to the property market.

Rather, in a syndicate you join with others to effectively take direct equity in one property (or occasionally two or more), which has been chosen for its appeal and potential.

Just like the solitary owner of a property, you have a say in the future of the investment, and you participate in all income distributions, all capital gains and all taxation benefits. Indeed, one of the key attractions for some investors is the sense of 'belonging' they achieve, having previously been involved in impersonal public syndicates with hundreds of members.

Public Syndicates and Private Syndicates

Many properties priced below $3 million tend to be bought by wealthy individuals, while the institutional buyers are mostly interested in properties priced over $15 million. Thus, there is virtually a vacuum between $3 million and $15 million, where you will find a serious shortage of buyers.

Some big property companies have stepped into this field, and specialise in buying one or two such properties, and then promote them to investors—via a prospectus lodged with the Australian Securities and Investments Commission—as public syndicates. Such opportunities are considered in detail in Chapter 22.

In this chapter, we shall discuss the growing number of small, informal, shared-property ventures being put together by lawyers, accountants, real estate agents and financial planners for their clients. By investing as little as $75,000 to $250,000 each, investors can collectively purchase substantial properties.

Table 18.1 highlights some differences between typical public and private syndicates.

Table 18.1: Differences Between Public and Private Syndicates

	PUBLIC SYNDICATES	PRIVATE SYNDICATES
Members	Often 200 to 300	No more than 20
Appointment of trustee	By the promoter	By the members
Choice of property	By the promoter	By the members
Initial costs	Establishment and acquisition costs, plus entrepreneurial and marketing fees	Establishment and acquisition costs only
Decision to sell	By the promoter	By the members
Regular updates	Usually generated by computer	Monthly statements, plus six-monthly personal briefings

The Profile of a Successful Private Syndicate

Syndicates can take various forms, but from Gardner+Lang's experience in structuring syndicated transactions for various clients since 1990, we have been able to come up with what we believe is a successful syndicate model.

Structure

Syndicates are generally best structured as unit trusts, unless members specifically request a joint venture form. Not only is a unit trust usually best for legal and taxation purposes, it also provides a shield against potential liability issues. (See Chapter 19 for detailed tables of the advantages and disadvantages of the various legal structures.)

Under Australian Securities and Investments Commission guidelines, each syndicate is to be limited to 20 investors, with the maximum combined equity to be contributed by them set at $2 million.

For ease of management, and to minimise the exposure for each individual syndicate member, a separate company can be incorporated as syndicate trustee—with a board of directors of two to three unitholders, appointed by the investors to ensure that their interests are properly protected.

The trustee then appoints a professional property management specialist to look after day-to-day matters, to make sure that the property is kept in good repair, and to ensure compliance with all regulatory and statutory requirements.

Borrowings

Total borrowings for each project should not usually exceed 65 per cent of the total purchase cost plus other expenses (such as minor renovations and the cost of finding tenants). This is intentionally conservative, and doesn't require any personal guarantees by you as an investor. And it means the income from the property should comfortably cover interest on the borrowings and all overheads.

Unless otherwise agreed, there should be no requirement for investors to provide any further capital, apart from their initial, upfront equity contribution. In addition, the syndicate should show a positive cash return to investors. However, this can vary if the syndicate wishes to renovate or improve the property, although the conservative nature of the initial borrowings will generally accommodate this without the need for investors to inject further equity.

Sale of Units

While there is be no public market in the units, there should be a provision in the trust deed for the transfer of units. Furthermore, a periodic, formal review of the syndicate by the members—say, every four years—should determine whether (and when) to sell the particular property.

If the majority wish to hold the property, but one or more syndicate members wishes to sell out, the trustee should have the power to increase the borrowings to buy back the units of those wishing to exit at that point.

Buying Criteria

Here are some suggested buying criteria. The property should:

- ⮱ be suitable for office, retail or industrial use
- ⮱ satisfy all legal and town-planning requirements
- ⮱ be reasonably new, and offer good depreciation allowances
- ⮱ have low ongoing maintenance
- ⮱ be of timeless or adaptable design, with the possibility for sub-division
- ⮱ not be of a specialised nature or unique design.

Clearly, modern conformity is the overriding consideration!

Preferred Locations

Properties should ideally be located within metropolitan areas, with preference to those in proven locations for that specific type of property (as determined by experts in the field)—usually no more than 15 to 20 minutes from the CBD (unless, of course, a syndicate is specifically put together for a regional growth area).

Excluded Properties

Because of the narrowness of their market, those properties of a speculative or specialised nature would be specifically ruled out. So, too, would any full-development proposals (which are basically investments in yet-to-be-built properties) which could expose the passive investor to unnecessary risks throughout the development period.

Price Range

Generally properties should be in the $3 million to $5 million range; other properties can be considered, if preferred by a particular syndicate.

Required Lease Terms

Each syndicate should strive for continuity of income. Thus, the following conditions are suggested:

➲ A target of at least five years remaining on the lease.

➲ Rentals need to be realistic—that is, at or below prevailing market rentals—with the opportunity for market reviews.

➲ In smaller properties, the majority of space should be occupied by a single tenant.

Due Diligence

As a condition of each purchase contract, qualified building consultants should conduct a due diligence report on all structural and technical aspects of the property. (A due diligence report confirms that a particular property has no impediments.) This will help minimise the risk of incurring any serious early maintenance, or replacement costs down the track.

Legal and Accounting Issues

Contracts should always be fully checked by lawyers and (if required) tax accountants, before a syndicate pays any deposit.

Timing of Investments into Each Syndicate

At the point of forming a syndicate, 30 per cent of your intended investment should be paid upfront into the syndicate. The trustee would then place the funds into a cash management account, so they are immediately available to meet the initial 10 per cent deposit on the purchase of the chosen property.

The remaining 70 per cent investment into the syndicate must then be paid within 28 days of the purchase contract being executed.

While an investment into a syndicate needs to be by way of cash, it need not all come out of your pocket. The financiers for the syndicate should also be able to provide personal funding (based upon equity investors may have in other property), in order that syndicate participants might improve their overall tax positions.

Yields

Yields should range from around 7 to 9 per cent, depending on the type and location of the property, the condition of the building, and (most importantly) the lease structure and stature of the tenant.

If all the conditions are right, investors should look to purchase at between a 7.5 per cent to 8.5 per cent yield, to achieve the ingredients necessary for a sound, long-term investment strategy. But this will change over time, depending upon the market for each type of property.

[Summary]

Syndicated property ownership is booming, and for a very simple reason: by joining with others you can buy a more attractive property than you can as an individual, while at the same time spreading your risk.

Syndicates can take many forms. In this chapter we have presented an outline of what we believe is an ideal syndicate, based on many years of experience in this field.

Now, in Chapter 19, let's look at some of the taxation benefits you can enjoy with commercial property investment.

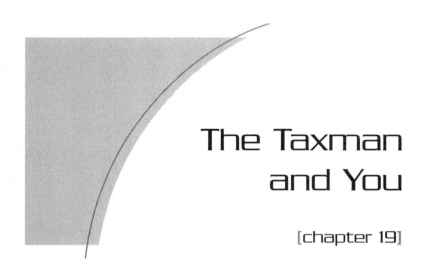

The Taxman
and You

[chapter 19]

Before you embark upon acquiring an investment property, it's vital that you get your affairs in order. And an important part of that is getting the right tax advice.

Minimising the Tax You Pay

The Australian Taxation Office (ATO) is quite happy for you to arrange your affairs to minimise the tax you pay. In other words, it is quite legal for you to avoid tax—you simply cannot evade it.

Income tax and capital gains tax are clearly two important issues to consider when arranging your property investments. But, tax planning is not the only factor to consider. There are other commercial concerns which, depending on your circumstances, you also need to address.

They include things such as:

- ➲ overall flexibility

- ➲ ability to admit partners down the track

- ➲ ability for one or more individuals to sell out when desired

- ➲ ability to cope with future tax changes

- ➲ ability to cope with a marriage breakdown

- ➲ ability to cope with the death of one or more individuals

- ➲ the ability to pass on the investments to future generations

- ➲ maximising the use of superannuation where desired.

If you haven't already done so, you should also give careful thought to these matters in choosing the best investment vehicle for you.

From a Tax Viewpoint, Which Vehicle is Best for You?

The simplest way to answer this question is to look at the advantages and disadvantages of a number of commonly recommended tax structures which might apply in your situation. The possible structures you might consider are a:

1. Company.

2. Fixed trust (commonly referred to as a unit trust).

3. Partnership or joint venture.

The advantages and disadvantages of each are outlined in the following three tables.

Table 19.1: Companies

ADVANTAGES	DISADVANTAGES
1. The company is a separate legal entity.	1. Can sometimes be complex to administer.
2. If the company's business fails, the personal assets of the shareholder are protected (asset protection).	2. Regulated by Corporations Law.
	3. Costly to establish.
	4. Costly to run.
3. Owners easily seem to understand how they operate.	5. 50% CGT discount not available.
4. Perpetual existence.	6. Cannot distribute losses to individuals.
5. The company can employ the taxpayer and provide salary packaging.	7. Complex rules regarding the carrying forward of losses.
6. By employing the taxpayer, the company can provide employer-sponsored superannuation and obtain maximum deductions compared to individuals and partnerships.	8. No easy way for a company to pass tax-free amounts to shareholders without them being taxed in the shareholders' hands.
7. It is easy to admit or retire partners by simply buying or selling shares, or alternatively by issuing shares.	9. Division 7A applies in respect of loans and other certain payments to shareholders.
8. A 30% flat rate of tax.	10. Income and capital cannot be distributed in a flexible manner. The anti-streaming and franking credit trading rules apply.
9. Shareholders have a fixed interest in the company so they can be certain of their entitlements.	
10. Franked dividends can be passed to shareholders, who can claim a refund of any excess imputation credits.	11. Supplies to associates for below market value consideration can be subject to GST.
11. Profits can be retained and taxed at the corporate tax rate when personal services income is not involved.	12. Directors can be personally liable for the company's debts in certain circumstances.
12. Buy-back rules are less restrictive these days.	13. The taxpayer must terminate their employment with the company in order to obtain the small business exemption.
13. A deduction may be claimed for interest on borrowings to pay tax or refinancing shareholders' loans or equity.	14. Share value shifting rules apply when issuing shares to associates on a non–arm's-length basis.
14. The substantiation rules do not apply.	15. Costly to wind up.

Table 19.2: Fixed Trusts

ADVANTAGES	DISADVANTAGES
1. Asset protection.	1. Fewer people understand how trusts operate.
2. Less regulation than a company.	2. Ultimate beneficiary statement rules apply.
3. The trust can employ the principals and provide salary packaging.	3. Complex PAYG calculation required for beneficiaries.
4. The trust can employ the principals and provide employer-sponsored superannuation.	4. More costly to establish and operate than a partnership of individuals.
5. No need to lodge returns and other forms with ASIC.	5. A change in unitholding can cause pre-CGT assets to become post-CGT assets.
6. The principals have a fixed interest which is good where independent parties are involved.	6. A change in asset holding can cause pre-CGT units to be taxed as post-CGT units.
7. The 50% CGT discount is available.	7. Complex trust loss rules apply.
8. There is no equivalent to the share value shifting rules.	8. Cannot transfer losses.
9. The trust is not taxed as a separate entity.	9. Cannot distribute losses to beneficiaries.
10. Loans from the trust are not subject to any special tax rules unless an unpaid present entitlement to a company exists at the time of the loan.	10. May need to elect to be a family trust. May not be able to elect to be a family trust.
11. It is less costly to wind up than a company.	11. No perpetual existence—normally must be wound up within 80 years.
12. Easy to admit new partners by issuing units, without CGT consequences.	12. Distribution of tax-free income and gains has CGT implications to the beneficiaries.
13. The substantiation rules do not apply.	13. Individual trustees can be personally liable for debts of the trust.
	14. Accumulated income taxed at top marginal rate (48.5%).
	15. If small business CGT retirement exemption is obtained, the principal must retire as an employee of the trust.
	16. If the trust is funded by debt, rather than equity, the units or interests owned by the beneficiaries will have a low cost base and this will cause problems where non-assessable amounts are distributed.
	17. If units in unit trusts are owned by discretionary trusts, the unit trust will not be able to satisfy the controlling individual test.

Table 19.3: Partnerships

ADVANTAGES	DISADVANTAGES
1. Less costly to establish than a company or a trust.	1. The partners are jointly and severally liable.
2. Inexpensive to run.	2. Generally no asset protection.
3. Can provide some flexibility in the partnership agreement.	3. Income cannot be accumulated and must be assessed at partners' tax rates.
4. Income splitting between partners.	4. Partners cannot claim input tax credits when paying partnership expenses.
5. Some tax planning possible with the use of 'partners' salaries'.	5. Complicated reimbursement procedure must be followed so that the partnership can claim the input tax credit under Division 111 GST Act.
6. Partners can obtain 50% CGT discount.	6. Partners cannot be employed by the partnership for salary packaging purposes.
7. Small business CGT concessions easily obtained.	7. Partners cannot claim a deduction for interest on borrowings to pay income tax, whereas individuals and other business entities can.
8. Partnership losses 'distributed' to partners to be offset against other income.	
9. Flexibility for CGT in that each partner can independently choose the concessions they want. Failure by one partner to satisfy the conditions will not affect the other partner.	
10. Flexibility and asset protection can be obtained by using trusts as partners.	
11. Independent parties can be easily admitted as partners.	
12. Trading stock and depreciable asset rollover relief available on the admission of partners.	
13. Tax planning opportunity available in respect of the refinancing of the partner's capital accounts by borrowed funds.	
14. No Division 7A type problems with debit loan accounts.	

As you will appreciate, volumes have been written on this topic. And so, with the help of Mike Williams[1] (of Williams Partners), we have tried to keep this explanation as simple and brief as possible. To correctly decide which structure is right for your needs, you should obtain specific advice from a tax accountant.

Tax Depreciation: A Waste of Time, or the Holy Grail?

With the expert help of Nicola Woodward[2] (of Apex Property Consulting), let's explore this vital topic in some detail.

There are many debates amongst investors as to the worth of tax depreciation. Some companies promise property investors huge tax deductions but fail to explain the future consequences of this. The secret lies in understanding their original purpose and matching that, and the many real benefits, with your investment strategy. We will discuss here the broad issues surrounding depreciation and investment properties.

Theoretically, the purpose of depreciation is to compensate taxpayers for the decline in value of depreciating assets (plant and equipment) over the effective life of those assets. The underlying assumption here is that your property and its components will decrease in value—you and the property market may however have other ideas! Therein lies the cause of the arguments.

---

1 Mike Williams heads up Williams Partners, an accounting firm servicing the specific needs of small to medium businesses and investors. You can contact Mike for further advice at: mikew@wp.com.au.

2 Nicola Woodward is a founding director of Apex Property Consulting, a boutique tax depreciation company which was established in 2002 to offer fully-integrated services to owners and managers of property portfolios, with a view to increasing value and reducing the risks inherent in property investment. You can contact Nicola at nwoodward@apexproperty.com.au if you need any further advice.

The truth is that the Treasury is not going to give significant tax deductions for a decline in value that doesn't occur! They are happy for you to take advantage of the provisions right up until you sell your property. But at that point, they require you to calculate what decline in value has actually occurred. If you have deducted more than the actual decline, then you effectively pay back that amount to the ATO—but in tomorrow's dollars.

This in itself is not a bad thing! Look at it this way: you buy a million dollar property in 2003 and hold it for 10 years. Over those years, you have total depreciation of $200,000, which comes off your assessable income, giving you an actual saving of $200,000 multiplied by your marginal tax rate, say 47 per cent, which equals $94,000. Much of this would be in the first three years of ownership.

After 10 years, you sell the property for $2 million. You will have a capital gain to pay on the land and buildings, along with a balancing adjustment to pay on the depreciating assets. Even if you have the same tax rate and end up paying back the $94,000 you will have the proceeds of the sale with which to do so and you will have had the cashflow advantage of the deductions during the ownership period.

If your marginal tax rate falls, you will be in an even better position on disposal—not to mention that $94,000 now is worth much more than $94,000 in 10 years time!

As long as you are aware of the consequences on disposal, you can plan for it and it won't come as a nasty surprise. The benefits of the depreciation in the early years will make your investment work harder for you, and your after-tax yield will look surprisingly healthy.

How Depreciation Actually Works

Capital allowances defer your payment of tax by reducing your assessable income, whether the asset is held by you as an individual or by a company, trust or superannuation fund. The ATO essentially recoups the deductions claimed through balancing adjustments and capital gains tax (CGT) when the asset is sold. Only the amount of the actual loss in value of the asset remains protected. However, you can gain substantial timing advantages by claiming the various allowable deductions.

Depreciating Your Plant and Equipment

Division 40 Capital allowances are available for capital expenditure incurred by you on plant and equipment (depreciating assets). They are based on the cost to you of acquiring the asset. Basically, this means you can depreciate:

- ➲ your assets at market value, or as a proportion of the acquisition cost (this is the most common for investment property);

- ➲ your assets at their written down value, or whatever other amount is stipulated in a contract; or

- ➲ the actual cost incurred to you of undertaking capital works (if you undertake a refurbishment or construction project).

Once you establish the cost base for each of your assets, a depreciation rate is applied to it in relation to:

- ➲ the effective life of the asset; and

- ➲ the method of depreciation, either prime cost (where depreciation occurs evenly over the effective life of the asset) or diminishing value (where the declining value for depreciation is assumed to be greatest in the first year, and smaller in each succeeding year).

In the year you buy your property, the available depreciation is pro-rated over the number of days you have owned it in that financial year. Figure 19.1 shows some depreciation rates.

Figure 19.1: Available Depreciation

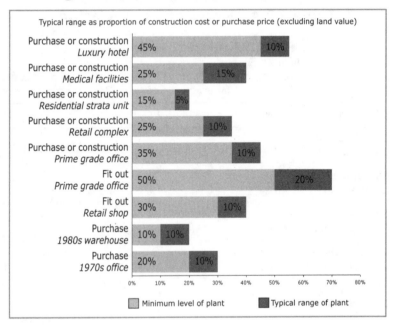

Depreciating the Building's Structural Component

Division 43 Capital works deductions, commonly known as building allowances, provide for taxpayers to write off certain capital expenditure incurred on the construction of income-producing buildings built, altered or refurbished after 21 August 1979. It is not uncommon for a single property to attract a number of different building allowances, due to phased construction, refurbishments and varying uses within the one building. (See the table overleaf for more details.)

Unlike capital allowances on depreciating assets, the building deductions are based on the historical construction cost of the eligible portion of the building. And this is where the services of quantity surveyors become worthwhile.

Table 19.4: Rates of Depreciation

	Hotels, Motels & Guest Houses	Manufact.	Other Comm.	Res.	Structural Improvements
27 Feb. 1992 –	4.0%	4.0%	2.5%	2.5%	2.5%
26 Feb. 1992 – 16 Sept. 1987	2.5%	2.5%	2.5%	2.5%	
15 Sept. 1987 – 18 July 1985	4.0%	4.0%	4.0%	4.0%	
17 July 1985 – 22 Aug. 1984	4.0%	4.0%	4.0%		
21 Aug. 1984 – 20 July 1982	2.5%	2.5%	2.5%		
19 July 1982 – 21 Aug. 1979	2.5%				

Why Take Advantage of Tax Depreciation?

Here are some good reasons to take advantage of tax depreciation:

➲ it improves your cashflow

➲ it defers the payment of your tax

➲ it gives you a good understanding of what you actually own

➲ it makes refurbishments and improvements far more affordable

➲ either you use it or you lose it.

[Summary]

Choosing the appropriate structure for your property acquisition can have a big impact on its overall performance. Read carefully the advantages and disadvantages of the three primary investment vehicles—company, fixed trust and partnership—but be aware that if you opt for one of these you will almost certainly need professional guidance.

Understanding taxation—particularly depreciation benefits and building allowances—is also crucial if you are to make the most of your investments. In many cases, it is possible to structure an investment to give you a positive cashflow, even with large mortgage payments.

In Chapter 20, the final chapter of Part II, we'll explore the importance of engaging a property manager for your property.

Working with a Property Manager

Choosing and buying a property might seem the hard part. But managing it also requires knowledge and application. A seemingly great investment, poorly managed, can end up losing—rather than making—you money.

In fact, a skilled property manager is becoming even more important as government legislation becomes increasingly more complex. For example, governments are introducing onerous new building regulations requiring building owners to assume responsibility for a wide range of 'essential services'. Few property investors have the experience—let alone the time— to keep up with such changes.

Here are some of the areas of knowledge your property manager needs to be conversant with:

1. Knowledge of the market and the marketplace:

⇨ rental levels in your property market

⇨ the balance of supply and demand in your market

⇨ history of the market, the properties, owners, tenants and service providers.

2. Knowledge of the laws governing ownership and leasing of real property:

⇨ land and tenant legislation

⇨ acts governing real estate agency practice

⇨ subdivision legislation

⇨ Essential Services Regulations

⇨ Dividing Fence Act

⇨ Local Government Act

⇨ lease preparation

⇨ rights of property owners

⇨ Trade Practices Act

⇨ Anti-Discrimination Act.

3. Knowledge of accountancy:

⇨ taxation advice in relation to repairs/replacements

⇨ income management

⇨ budget forecasting

⇨ basic bookkeeping principles

⇨ mortgage finance

⇨ insurance.

4. *Knowledge of various authorities concerned with:*

⇨ town planning

⇨ building codes of Australia

⇨ fire regulations

⇨ health and safety matters.

5. *Knowledge of construction:*

⇨ building methods

⇨ costing

⇨ alternative materials

⇨ design and decoration

⇨ market requirements

⇨ optimum layouts

⇨ property maintenance.

So what does a property manager do? Here are some of the duties and responsibilities you should expect your professional manager to look after:

➲ your property is always let to good tenants

➲ those tenants pay their rental by the due date

- ➲ your property is well cared for

- ➲ any maintenance would be fully detailed and carried out cost effectively, but always with quality workmanship

- ➲ all maintenance is undertaken by reliable tradespeople

- ➲ you would be notified well before each tenancy becomes vacant

- ➲ every possible step is taken to re-let the property

- ➲ your rentals are reviewed at appropriate intervals, to reflect a fair market rent

- ➲ timely payment of any outgoings occurs on your behalf

- ➲ your monthly statement and rental cheque are sent to you promptly

- ➲ you receive accurate advice on any insurance requirements

- ➲ your property is regularly inspected

- ➲ your property is kept competitive in the marketplace.

In fact, a good manager does immeasurably more. He or she ought to be your partner in ensuring that the value of the property as an investment is maintained and enhanced. That's why it is often the more imperceptible elements that are the key to the relationship between owner and manager—such elements as a professional attitude and efficient communication procedures.

Most real estate agencies offer a property management service. However, for many of these agencies it is a sideline to their mainstream business of selling and leasing properties. Indeed, for many of the high fliers in the real estate business, property management is dull and predictable, in comparison to the adrenalin rush they can receive from a big sale or letting. That's why it is often better, when you seek a professional property manager, to give preference to someone for whom management is a mainstream business.

Developing a firm relationship with an experienced property manager can provide you with a host of benefits. The manager is out there in the marketplace, constantly interacting with owners and tenants. Very likely it is the manager, rather than the real estate salesperson, who is first to know that a particular property deal is in the wind.

Questions to Ask a Property Manager

So, knowing the vital importance of a skilled and experienced property manager, what questions do you ask to help you determine that he or she is well-organised, competent and able to deliver to you the level of service you need as a serious investor?

Here are 17 probing questions to ask your intended property manager:

To find out about your property manager's mindset:

1. What are the underlying precepts which determine a top-class property manager?

2. What are the key principles a competent property manager should operate by?

3. What principles ensure a lasting relationship between owner and manager?

Your best safeguard—an astute property manager's self-interest:

4. What are the two main reasons why a properly structured property management portfolio should be viewed as the lifeblood of their business?

Step behind the scenes. Ask the property manager:

5. Exactly what it is they do for you?

6. Can they give you specific standards by which they measure their performance?

7. How do they ensure that these standards are actually met?

8. What is their system for controlling late payers?

Find out how much they know! What is the extent of the property manager's knowledge in the areas of:

9. The market and the marketplace?

10. Taxation (especially the GST and capital gains tax)?

11. The laws governing ownership and leasing of property?

12. Trust accounting?

13. Various legislative requirements?

14. Building and construction?

Find out about essential services (new building regulations). You need to protect yourself:

15. When was the last Essential Services Inspection carried out?

16. Did the manager provide a copy of that inspection report?

17. Have identified breaches been rectified?

Some Frequently Asked Questions

What costs are involved in property management?

That generally depends upon the size and type of property involved. For example: the fee for a small, strata office would be around 6 per cent (plus GST) of monies collected; for a large, brand-new industrial property (where the tenant is on a full-maintenance lease), your fee may be as low as 2 per cent.

What type of contract would you normally enter into?

For a straightforward smaller property, the standard Real Estate Institute Management Authority will usually suffice. But for a complex building, with multiple tenants, you are better served by a more formal contract.

What if you find you are unhappy with your manager?

Generally, you will give the manager a reasonable period (say, 30 days) to remedy any oversight, before taking steps to terminate. Some agreements do have a standing three-month notice period by either party.

[Summary]

Not a lot of commercial property assets are truly 'let and forget'. Most investments do need to be properly managed. Nowadays, that means a lot more than collecting the rent each month.

Ever-changing government legislation means that the owner of a property has many legal obligations to a tenant, particularly in the field of essential services. For this reason, most investors in commercial property will want to use the services of an experienced property manager. In this chapter we have attempted to outline the duties of a manager, and some of the questions you need to ask potential managers.

This chapter concludes Part II—Direct Property Investment. In Part III, we shall cover other forms of property investment, starting with listed property trusts.

Part III
Other Property
Investments

The Changing World of Listed Property Trusts

As you're probably already aware, listed property trusts are pooled investments that are listed on the Australian Stock Exchange. They invest in a wide range of commercial property assets, and own many of Australia's main office buildings and shopping centres, as well as a growing number of industrial and leisure properties.

The trust manager chooses properties for the portfolio, and is then responsible for their maintenance and renovation, and for collecting rentals. Investors, like you, buy and sell units in the trusts through a stockbroker—in the same manner that you buy and sell equities. Trust prices are published by the exchange in the same way as regular share prices, and are available through many online stockbroking services as well as in daily newspapers. Appendix D contains a table from the ASX showing property trust performance.

Investors receive dividends—called distributions—usually every three or six months. As owners of the properties, investors also benefit from gains in their value. The trusts do not pay taxation, so are unable to offer franking credits, although there are other taxation benefits for investors.

How Listed Trusts Developed

Listed property trusts evolved from the debacle of the early 1990s, when property prices fell and many unlisted property trusts found themselves unable to meet investor demands to redeem their holdings. Sadly, some of these investors had lost money in the 1987 stock market crash, and had switched to property thinking it to be a safe haven.

Initially it was thought that they might develop on the US pattern, with a trust for every conceivable sector, from mobile home parks to household storage property. However, this did not eventuate. There also proved to be a lack of demand for development trusts, in which investors placed money into a trust right at the start of a building project, and had to wait a year or so before receiving any return.

Listed trusts have become by far the most popular means for the smaller investor to access commercial property, and the Property Trust sector of the stock market has enjoyed powerful growth, from a market capitalisation of under $5 billion in the early 1990s to more than $48 billion in mid-2003, making it the fourth-largest ASX sector.

Recent Developments

At the end of the 1990s, with equities looking vulnerable, a lot of new institutional money started to flow into the trusts.

The institutions preferred the bigger, more liquid trusts, and so the thinking developed among some trust managers that growth was vital. But with a scarcity of high-quality new investment properties, there was only moderate scope for expansion, and the result was a steady trend towards mergers and acquisitions within the industry.

Many of the trusts also began expanding their investments overseas. They have been especially attracted to America, a huge market with commercial property available at yields of up to 9.5 per cent. Such is the concentration now that, in mid-2003, the four largest property trusts represented more than half the entire sector market capitalisation. Below are the top ten.

Table 21.1: Top 10 Property Trusts
(July 2003)

Market Capitalisation*	
Westfield Trust	7.7
Westfield America Trust	7.3
General Property Trust	5.9
Stockland Trust Group	5.6
Mirvac Group	3.0
CFS Gandel Retail Trust	2.5
Centro Properties Group	2.2
Investa Property Group	1.7
Macquarie Goodman Industrial Trust	1.7
Commonwealth Property Office Fund	1.7

(* in $ billions)

Types of Trusts

Many of the trusts are diversified, with interests that span a huge range. For example, two of the largest of these, General Property Trust and Stockland Trust Group, own some of Australia's biggest shopping centres and office buildings, along with industrial parks and hotels. The retail sub-sector also includes some major entities, notably Westfield Trust—Australia's largest listed property trust —which owns major shopping complexes throughout Australia and New Zealand. Other big retail trusts include Centro Properties Group and CFS Gandel Retail Trust.

The office trust sub-sector is dominated by Investa Property Group (formerly Westpac Property Trust) and Commonwealth Property Office Fund, with investments in prime office properties around Australia. The industrial sub-sector is considerably smaller than the others. The largest is Macquarie Goodman Industrial Trust, which specialises in business parks, industrial estates and warehouse/ distribution centres, in Sydney, Melbourne and New Zealand.

A number of hotel groups have structured themselves as property trusts. The largest (though they're small compared to many other listed trusts) are Thakral Holdings, which owns hotels in several Australian cities and also develops hotel apartments, and Grand Hotel Group, which owns 25 Hyatt, Chifley and Country Comfort hotels. Two major overseas property trusts are Westfield America Trust (one of Australia's largest listed trusts), which owns a fast-growing portfolio of American shopping malls, and Lend Lease US Office Trust, which invests in prime American commercial buildings.

As the trusts increasingly encounter difficulties in finding a sufficient number of high-grade properties to add to their portfolios, expect them to diversify into a growing number of niche areas, such as health care and retirement properties, or sub-sectors of current sectors, such as high-tech industrial properties and bulky goods retail properties.

Performance

The listed property trust sector has been an excellent long-term performer, on a par with—or better than—the All Ordinaries Index itself (see below). Indeed, as investors generally sold down equities in the period after the 'tech-wreck' of early 2000, there were strong moves into listed property.

Figure 21.1: **Annualised Total Returns**
(March 2003)

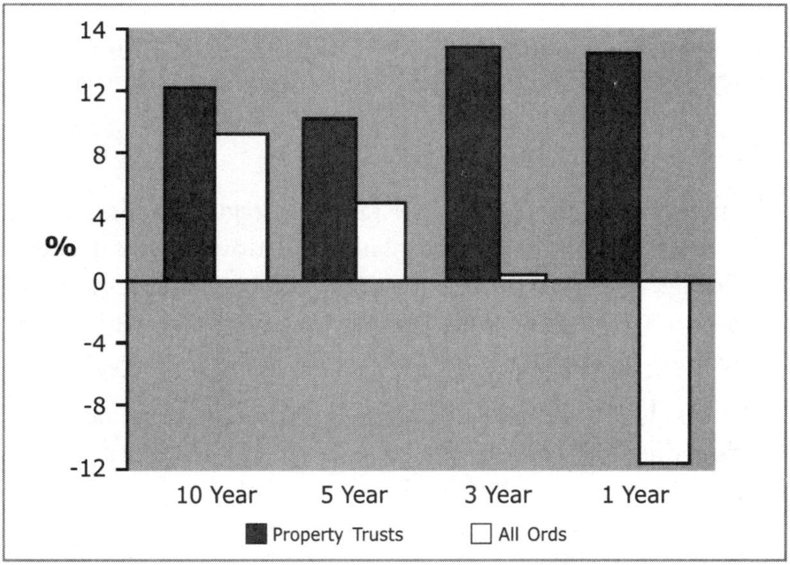

Source: Data derived from Australian Stock Exchange.

Advantages of Property Trusts

The main attractions of listed property trusts, and the reason that they have become so popular among small investors, are that they are highly liquid and provide the opportunity of investing in a professionally managed portfolio of quality commercial property at a reasonable entry fee. But they offer lots more.

High Yields

Listed property trusts have, on average, delivered historical yields ranging between 7 and 9 per cent. This is higher than for any other stock market sector, and is roughly double the average for the entire market. It also compares favourably with returns from residential property.

The reason for the high yields is that trusts pay out all their profit (which is the rental they receive from their properties, minus their costs) as distributions (dividends) to unitholders. They do not retain profits for future capital expenditure.

Taxation Benefits

Property trusts offer investors a tax-advantaged component of the distribution, from depreciation allowances on their buildings. However, though attractive, this benefit is not usually as advantageous to investors as franking credits related to the dividends for shares.

There is also a tax-deferred component, thanks to other taxation deductions. This component can be as much as 100 per cent of the total distribution. Because it is deferred, investors do not pay tax on this portion of the distribution until they sell their units in the trust, and then at the concessional capital gains tax rate.

Cost

You can invest in property trusts with as little as around $1,000, or even less, though broking fees can make a small investment uneconomical.

Gearing

After a slow start, most trusts have taken advantage of recent years of low interest rates in Australia to gear themselves with borrowed funds, in order to expand their portfolios.

High debt levels contributed to the failure of several trusts in the early 1990s, with the result that by 1996 the average gearing ratio was only about 5 per cent. It has since risen to around 20 to 30 per cent.

Clearly debt management skills are now an important consideration in the trust business, with borrowings enabling managers to buy more properties and better properties, and to diversify. But there is the concern that low interest rates may encourage trust managers to borrow simply in order to achieve growth—and at the same time boost their management fees— with the possibility of acquiring properties of less than the highest quality. This is at a time when there are complaints within the industry that Australia has a shortage of quality major properties.

The ability to achieve returns higher than mortgage rates has been a significant factor in the recent strong performance of property trusts. But of course, should interest rates rise, it could turn out to be a negative. As a result, much borrowing is hedged.

A commentary in *Property Journal* in October 1998 said simply:

> Some believe that there will be increasing differentiation between the managers who have appropriate [debt management] skills and those who do not. This will ultimately be reflected in the price of the trust units—and, perhaps, the survival of some managers.

Information Flow

There is a huge amount of information available about the leading trusts, and a lot about most of the others. As they are listed on the stock exchange, each trust must issue a prospectus and provide an annual report. These are often extremely comprehensive. Most of the trust companies have websites with more detail. In addition, because property trusts are such a significant part of the stock market, broking houses regularly prepare sector analyses and reports for their clients.

Several independent information providers, such as Property Investment Research, also offer regular analysis of the sector, primarily for the benefit of financial planners, though anyone can access their output.

Indeed, with an estimated 50 or so analysts covering the sector —working for stockbrokers, fund managers and research houses —there have been some suggestions that property trusts are over-analysed.

Diversification

Though some trusts are formed to invest in just one or a few buildings, most are invested across a number of properties. It gives small investors access to a range of properties, and also gives protection should problems arise with one property. This places them in contrast to property syndicates, which are generally invested in just one property, or, occasionally, two or three.

Disadvantages of Property Trusts

There are of course some disadvantages to property trusts.

Lack of Control

As a small investor, you will have little say in the management of the trust. Most investors, of course, desire no control whatsoever. But it could be that the trust managers choose to buy a property you consider undesirable, or to sell a property you believe they should keep. Or they may take some other action you think inappropriate. There's not much you can do about it. As already noted in this book, some recent corporate collapses have demonstrated that the management of public companies is not always working in the best interests of shareholders.

Volatility

Listed property trusts are less volatile than most equities, but more volatile than an investment in direct property. This can actually work in favour of the astute investor, who might be able to buy a trust shortly before the share price accelerates. But it can also make it possible to buy shortly before the price goes into a long period of hibernation. This, of course, is a particular risk for small investors, who too often buy shares that are receiving publicity, and which may have reached their peaks.

Volatility adds to the risk, making property trusts more risky, in theory, than a direct property investment. Nevertheless, the high liquidity of property trusts means that it is possible to get out of the investment quickly if something goes wrong, which is not usually the case with direct property.

Lack of a Strong Correlation to Direct Property

Investors buy property trusts in order to gain exposure to commercial property, yet share prices of the trusts do not necessarily move in line with property prices, as noted already in Chapter 2.

Property trusts are basically stock market investments, and are highly influenced by market trends. When the authorities decide to inject liquidity into the economy by cutting interest rates, it can have an immediate and favourable impact on the market, including the trusts, while taking much longer to filter through to actual property values.

The trusts may also be bought by investors looking for a safe haven when other stock market investments are looking dangerous.

For all these reasons the correlation to property values is often tenuous.

Investing in Property Trusts

Property Investment Research advises that potential investors check the following:

- ➲ What is the quality of the underlying property assets?

- ➲ What is the track record and capacity of the trust manager to add value?

- ➲ How secure is the income stream (for example, what are the lease terms and rent review details)?

- ➲ What returns can I expect from my LPT investment?

- ➲ What risks are involved in a particular LPT investment?

- ➲ Is my current research and advice independent?

- ➲ Does market sentiment favour this LPT's price at the moment?

- ➲ Is the sector currently in an uptrend, consolidating, or in a downtrend?

It is easy to buy shares in a listed property trust. All you need is an account with a stockbroker, and you simply place an order. You will of course incur a stockbroking fee. Thus, it would not normally be considered economical to place an order worth less than, say, $1,000. For example, if you were to buy just $500 of shares, you need a return of 6 per cent just to recoup a broking fee of $30.

You will receive a distribution generally twice or four times a year. Increasingly, companies are sending an annual statement to help you with tax planning. Some trusts operate a distribution reinvestment plan, by which you can reinvest your distribution in more units, usually at a small discount to the prevailing market price, and without broking fees.

The trust manager takes a fee, which is normally expressed as a percentage of the total assets. Typically it is around 0.5 per cent of the assets. Some trusts may have a provision giving the managers a performance fee, if shares in the trust perform to a certain benchmark.

For example, General Property Trust announced in early 2003 a new fee structure. It cut the fee from 0.55 per cent of gross assets to 0.4 per cent, but with the addition of a performance fee equal to 5.0 per cent of the trust's total return above the S&P/ASX Property 200 Accumulation Index (capped at 0.55 per cent of gross assets).

About a dozen trusts are part of a 'stapled' securities structure, whereby investors own units in the trust and also shares in another security. The latter security is typically a funds management company, usually responsible for managing the trust and its properties as well as for other development activities. The units and the shares cannot be traded separately. Investing in trusts with a stapled security attached generally involves higher risk, but can also bring additional returns.

Monitoring Property Trusts

The Australian Stock Exchange classifies all listed companies into sectors, based upon the Global Industry Classification Standard (GICS) devised by Standard & Poor's—who administer the sector indices—with Morgan Stanley Capital International, the world's two major providers of equity index services. The GICS is aimed at easing the investment research and management process for financial professionals worldwide, and was developed to facilitate sector analysis and investing on a global basis.

In other countries, property trusts are included within the financials sector. However, it was felt that in Australia property trusts are generally treated as a separate asset class to equity, and with levels of gearing lower than elsewhere in the world. The result is separate sectoral indices for property trusts. The most-used one is the S&P/ASX 200 Property Trust Index, which is formed from the 29 property trusts that are included among the 200 largest listed companies.

The stockbroking firm UBS-Warburg Australia produces a considerable amount of research material on the sector, and it also compiles six of its own sub-sector indices, covering trust leaders as well as diversified trusts, retail trusts, commercial (office) trusts, industrial trusts and hotel trusts. Some other broking houses also compile their own property trust indices.

Property Trust Futures

The Australian Stock Exchange has introduced the ASX Mini 200 Property Trusts futures contract. The underlying index of this contract is the S&P/ASX 200 Property Trusts sector index.

[Summary]

Listed property trusts are by far the most popular route into commercial property for the smaller investor, and they have become one of the major stock market sectors. Trusts offer the opportunity of accessing some of Australia's property icons for a modest investment outlay. Other benefits include their liquidity, professional management, high yields and taxation advantages. But investors do need to understand that their performance is often more related to stock exchange movements than to actual property price trends.

Another form of pooled property investment—public property syndicates—has also recently been enjoying a boom in investor popularity, and you will learn more about them in the next chapter.

A Look at Public Property Syndicates

Public property syndicates are similar to listed property trusts in many respects. Professional syndicate managers pool the money of investors to buy commercial real estate, which they manage. Rental income, minus costs, is distributed to investors, generally on a quarterly or half-yearly basis.

But there are some important differences with property trusts. The syndicates are usually formed for a fixed period—typically around 5 to 10 years—to buy a fixed property (or number of properties).

A characteristic public syndicate has a size of $20 million to $30 million. At the end of the term of the syndicate, the property is sold, and investors receive any capital gains. In some cases, the syndicates are rolled over into a new syndicate, to help investors avoid capital gains tax.

As the syndicates are not listed on the stock exchange, it is difficult—if not impossible—for investors to trade property syndicate holdings, or to know the precise current value of their investment.

The public syndicates are of course similar to private syndicates, discussed in Chapter 18. However, there are differences that are summarised in the table on page 137.

Public property syndicates have enjoyed exceptional expansion in recent years, with heightened investor interest being matched by a range of new investment opportunities, including the entry to this market of some major financial institutions. In mid-1998, less than $1 billion was invested in public syndicates. By mid-2003, the figure was around $9 billion.

Industry research indicates that the average syndicate investor is 10 years older than the average listed property trust investor, that the average investment is around $35,000 and that some 30 to 40 per cent of funds come from DIY superannuation funds.

Advantages of Public Property Syndicates

High Returns

Skilled property syndicate managers choose their properties carefully, and many are able to offer yields of 8.5 to 10.0 per cent, a little higher than the average for property trusts. This yield is, of course, not guaranteed. Much depends on the ability of the manager to find the right tenants for the duration of the investment. But when it goes right, the returns can be impressive, with a healthy capital gain also possible at the termination of the syndicate.

But exercise caution. It doesn't always go right. Some public syndicates have been unable to meet their rosy forecasts.

For example, when the supermarket chain Franklins closed down it hurt several syndicates.

Taxation Advantages

Property syndicates offer taxation advantages—notably depreciation allowances—that are similar to those of property trusts. Indeed, in the early years of a syndicate, when depreciation allowances may be at their highest, it is sometimes possible for most distributions to be effectively free of tax.

Gearing

Property syndicates are generally more highly geared than property trusts, with gearing ratios (debt as a percentage of assets) around 50 to 65 per cent. In an environment of low interest rates this clearly gives them the potential for higher returns. This is one of the reasons they have been outperforming listed property trusts, and one of the factors that has attracted many new investors to them.

Valuations

The value of the investment is tied directly to property prices. Property syndicates—unlike listed property trusts—are not subject to the volatility of the stock market. For investors seeking to diversify a portfolio with property, a syndicate is far more reflective of actual property values than are listed trusts.

Disadvantages of Public Property Syndicates

Cost

Property syndicates generally have minimum investment amounts, typically $5,000 to $10,000. Though this is, of course, substantially less than buying your own property, it is a lot more than is needed to invest in a listed property trust.

Fixed Term

Investors are generally locked into the investment for the life of the syndicate, with few means of getting out. If everything goes smoothly, this is not a problem. But if problems develop with the syndicate, or your investment objectives change, or you urgently need money, your options are limited.

A fixed term also means that the end of the life of the syndicate —when the property is to be sold, and the proceeds distributed to investors—could coincide with a property downturn. This could mean little capital gain or, even, a capital loss. Partly for this reason, some syndicates contain provisions giving the manager the power to wind it up early, or to delay the sale of the property. Some syndicates have a provision that allows it to be rolled over for a new term.

The Bendigo Stock Exchange and the Austock Exempt Property Market both facilitate trading in a small range of property syndicates, but volumes are tiny. Plans are under way to launch an Australian Property Exchange, which has the potential to inject liquidity into the syndicate market.

Debt Levels

The high gearing level of syndicates has been cited as one of their attractions, because it can help generate higher returns. Although borrowings will often be locked in at fixed rates, this may not always be the case. It is necessary for investors to check whether the syndicate would suffer if interest rates were to rise substantially.

Lack of Diversification

Most syndicates are invested in one or two properties only. If problems develop—for example, an anchor tenant decides not to renew a lease at a shopping centre that is owned by the syndicate—the impact can be huge. And because they are usually formed to invest in a specified asset, they cannot move into new properties, even where these might boost returns.

High Fees

Apart from normal acquisition and property management costs, establishment fees—which include marketing costs—can be as much as 4 to 5 per cent of your investment. An annual management fee is also charged, typically 0.4 to 0.6 per cent of the value of the property, and the managers might also take a percentage of the property's income. In addition, there is often an exit fee, which can be 2 to 4 per cent of the final value of the property, and might be linked to the performance of the investment.

Scarcity of Information

Some investors complain that listed property trusts are over-analysed. Not so with property syndicates. Occasional articles appear in the financial and business media, but otherwise most of the analysis of syndicates comes from specialist firms, and is not easily accessible by smaller private investors. For this reason, much investment in public property syndicates is done through financial advisers.

Size

Some investors find comfort in the size and impersonal of the public property syndicates. Yet for others this i of frustration. Investors in a public syndicate—as in a listed property trust—have very little say in the management of the property.

By contrast, the much smaller, private syndicates (which are covered in Chapter 18) sometimes provide members with the opportunity to work actively with an experienced property manager throughout the entire cycle of selecting, acquiring, managing and then marketing a particular property. Not only can this give you a strong sense of satisfaction and a true feeling of ownership, it is also the ideal way to educate yourself about the workings of the commercial property market.

The Property Syndicate Companies

In mid-2003, more than 40 companies were involved in the public property syndication business. Some had only minimal amounts—less than $50 million—under management, and many experts were forecasting a looming shakeout within the industry, with a round of mergers and takeovers possible.

At the time of writing the leading syndicators included:

➲ Centro MSC—its mid-2003 acquisition of MCS Property made Centro Properties Group by far the largest property syndicator in Australia, with $2.3 billion of assets. The new entity was to be named Centro MSC. ⌐ ̄ ̄ ⌐ had held the number one rank, due to ⌐ of a stream of syndicates, devoted ⌐ing centres. Centro also manages listed ⌐ and thanks to the MSC acquisition it ⌐ralia's second-largest owner of shopping ⌐stfield Trust.

⮚ Macquarie Direct Property is part of Macquarie Bank and has established a series of syndicates invested in commercial, retail and industrial property in New South Wales. In 2002 it was responsible for Australia's largest-ever syndicate offering, the Martin Place Trust, which raised more than $100 million for a 50 per cent share of a Sydney office tower.

⮚ Australian Unity has grown through takeover. Like Macquarie Direct, it has more than $500 million worth of property under management.

⮚ Investa Property Group is one of Australia's largest specialist commercial property managers. It is steadily building a large portfolio of syndicated property, specialising in office assets.

Investing in a Property Syndicate

The key point about an investment in a public property syndicate is that you are buying into a single asset (or occasionally two or several). So it is crucial that you trust the syndicate promoter's ability to, firstly, choose a property with good income and the potential for capital gain, and, secondly, manage that property well for the life of the investment.

Here are other points to consider:

⮚ Check if independent research is available about the syndicate. Firms such as Property Investment Research and Lonsdale Securities prepare reports on many individual syndicates. Financial advisers often have access to these.

⮚ Are the fees in line with industry norms? Or are they excessively high, which could have an impact on your own returns? Or unexpectedly low, which might even suggest an inexperienced manager?

⊃ If you are placing the investment in your superannuation fund, check that the syndicate is structured appropriately.

⊃ Make sure you carefully read what the prospectus has to say about likely income, capital appreciation and taxation benefits. What are the assumptions used for these forecasts? Do these assumptions accord with reality?

⊃ Is the property as well-maintained as the prospectus says? Is it housed with quality tenants? What unexpected costs might arise?

⊃ Look at the level and manner of gearing. What might happen if interest rates were to rise?

Summary

Public property syndicates are enjoying an enormous boom in popularity, as investors come to appreciate their attractions. Like listed property trusts, they are professionally managed, but generally offer higher returns. And unlike the listed trusts—whose prices can fluctuate quite substantially, in line with stock market trends—valuations tend to conform directly with property values. However, they are rather illiquid investments, and are usually invested in just one property only.

In Chapter 23, the final chapter of this book, we shall examine a range of other property investments, including property securities funds and mortgage funds.

More Property
Investment
Opportunities

Property Securities Funds

These are unit trusts (managed funds) that invest in a basket of listed property trusts (see Chapter 21 for more on listed property trusts), and, sometimes, directly in property assets. Investors buy via a prospectus. The funds have shown strong growth, along with the expansion of the listed property trust industry.

Property securities funds have proven attractive to conservative investors wishing to include property trusts in their long-term portfolios—perhaps as part of a self-managed superannuation fund—but who do not know much about the sector.

The largest funds are Deutsche Paladin Property Securities and APN Property for Income Fund, each of which in mid-2003 managed assets of more than $500 million.

Advantages of Property Securities Funds

Many investors wishing to add a listed property component to their portfolios really have no idea where to start. The funds are especially suited to them. In theory, skilled fund managers choose a selection of trusts offering the best potential, and invest only in those. They will also, to a certain extent, time the market, reducing and increasing exposure to different areas of the market. Most private investors do not have the knowledge or experience (or desire) to do this.

Disadvantages of Property Securities Funds

Investors will effectively be paying double fees—to both the property trust management and to the securities fund management. And the evidence suggests that most funds—despite the high salaries paid to many fund management teams—struggle to beat the listed property trust averages.

In addition, there is not a lot of information available about these funds, other than from the fund managers themselves and a limited number of research houses. Most investors will likely buy into the funds via a financial adviser.

But it is another issue that could make property securities funds a dubious proposition. Recent years have seen a wave of consolidation within the listed property trust sector. The number of trusts has been falling, while their average size has been increasing. The result is that an investment in, say, General Property Trust means that your money is invested across a huge spread of quality property that includes some of Australia's leading office towers and shopping centres, along with industrial estates, business parks and hotels. If you believe the General Property Trust management is competent, then there seems little point in paying extra fees to invest in a property securities fund, just for the sake of diversity.

Indeed, such is the concentration now (mid-2003) within property trusts that buying units in the four largest of them—Westfield Trust, Westfield America Trust, General Property Trust and Stockland Trust Group—means that you are invested in half the sector (by market capitalisation).

Unlisted Property Trusts

Most mainstream property trusts are now publicly listed. Those that remain unlisted are generally wholesale funds, for institutional investors. However, some are open to retail investors, though due to liquidity concerns these often maintain large cash holdings and may also have part of their investment in listed property trusts. Thus, they are actually very similar to property securities funds. Several others are in niche areas of the market, such as the Australian Unity Healthcare Property Trust.

Mortgage Trusts

These are funds which invest in commercial or residential property mortgages. They offer regular returns that have a high gearing to interest rates. Investments are made through a prospectus. The largest of the funds are Howard Mortgage Trust and Colonial First State Income, each of which in mid-2003 managed more than $1 billion.

Some funds invest mainly in mortgages with fixed interest rates, which makes them attractive in an environment of falling rates (and unattractive when rates rise). Others invest mainly in mortgages with variable rates. Several aim to boost returns by investing in development projects.

In mid-2003, mortgage funds were providing yields of around 4.5 to 6.5 per cent (which will obviously change over time).

Advantages of Mortgage Trusts

Most investors are attracted to mortgage funds for their security, with returns underwritten by property holdings. They have low volatility, and their yields are comparable to cash management trusts or fixed term deposits.

Disadvantages of Mortgage Trusts

Liquidity can be an issue. It may not be possible to get back your investment quickly, should you so require. Many funds now have substantial cash holdings, in order to meet redemptions, but they may still require that investors wait for a certain period—as long as two months—before receiving back their money.

The underlying assets of the funds are mortgages, so they offer income, but no capital growth.

Recent years of low interest rates and a strong economy have made mortgage funds a secure investment. But it must not be forgotten that should interest rates rise, and the economy slow, the funds could be hit by defaults.

Mezzanine Finance

Mezzanine finance is a term used to describe the intermediate level of funding for property development—between equity and debt, and with characteristics of each—and is an emerging and growing opportunity for Australian investors.

As an example, a property developer might have available, say, 10 or 20 per cent of the funds needed for a new project. This is the developer's own equity in the scheme. A bank will be prepared to lend typically 60 to 70 per cent of the finance needed. Thus, mezzanine financing is needed to provide the remaining 10 to 30 per cent.

In essence, it is a loan from private investors at a higher rate of interest than the bank charges, and sometimes with a second mortgage over the property.

The advantage for developers is that they are able to borrow substantially more than the 60 per cent to 70 per cent that the banks are normally comfortable lending at preferential interest rates.

Investors receive higher returns than on many other investments: yields of 10 to 20 per cent are possible, and even higher for more speculative ventures. Often there is provision for investors to share in any capital gains from the project. Investment terms are typically one to three years.

Mezzanine finance, a relatively new business in Australia for smaller investors, is arranged by specialist managers with expertise in property. Until recently it was the preserve of high-worth individuals, with a minimum investment of $500,000 sometimes required. However, some specialist financial planners and property consultants are starting to put together schemes in which smaller investors—those with $5,000 or more—can place funds.

There are risks. The main one is of course a failure of the project, in which case the providers of mezzanine finance have to wait until all bank borrowings are repaid before becoming entitled to any return. It is also crucial to check the credentials of the promoters of a mezzanine finance project, to ensure they have experience and ability. Be clear, too, about the nature of the scheme. Ensure that your money is for a specific project, with a specific, secured return.

This is an illiquid investment. Investors cannot usually withdraw their money until the end of the term of the project.

The Australian Securities and Investments Commission carries a special paper on the risks of mezzanine finance at its website (www.fido.asic.gov.au/fido/fido.nsf/byheadline/Mezzanine+investing+and+2+golden+rules?openDocument).

It concludes:

> Mezzanine investing may really suit only experienced investors who know the property scene, understand the project seeking money and know and trust the people involved. Every deal will be different. You need skill, care and patience to find the right ones.

Infrastructure Investments

As noted in Chapter 3, the politics of economic rationalism has led to a stream of new infrastructure projects being placed in private hands, and the privatisation of many public assets. The result is a new wave of investment opportunities in such properties as highways, power plants, airports and ports.

Many of the investments are available in the form of infrastructure trusts, sometimes with stapled securities attached, so that investors can benefit from both the development and ongoing operations of the project.

With stable and fairly predictable revenues, like property trusts, these investments are particularly suited for conservative investors, and those looking for income more than capital gain.

The best-known listed infrastructure investments are:

➲ Australian Infrastructure Fund—invests in a wide sweep of properties, including airports, ports, toll roads, railway assets and utilities. It provides the most diversified exposure of all the investments.

⮕ Hills Motorway Group—built and manages the M2 motorway in Sydney.

⮕ Macquarie Airports—invests in airports around the world.

⮕ Macquarie Communications Infrastructure Group—a new company formed to invest primarily in broadcast infrastructure properties within OECD countries.

⮕ Macquarie Infrastructure Group—a major investor in toll roads in Australia, Europe and the US. It also has an electric power station investment.

⮕ Prime Infrastructure Group—a new group that owns Queensland's Dalrymple Bay coal terminal and also has power station holdings.

⮕ Transurban Group—runs Melbourne's CityLink toll road, and also has interests in many other road projects around the world.

Advantages of Infrastructure Investments

As noted already in Chapter 3, infrastructure investments tend to be very stable. By their nature, they usually operate in a monopoly—or highly protected—environment, providing essential services. As long as the economy remains firm, it is reasonable to expect that revenues will be maintained, on a fairly predictable basis. In fact, they should grow, along with the economy.

Thus, like property trusts, infrastructure properties can make excellent investments for investors looking for a steady stream of dividends with a relatively low level of risk. There is also the prospect of some capital gain, as the economy grows and also as the company diversifies into other projects.

Disadvantages of Infrastructure Investments

The huge costs of a project mean that infrastructure companies typically have very high debts. During the construction phase they have little income, so may be unable to pay out anything to their shareholders. And during the initial period of operations, heavy debt repayments might limit dividends. Also, due to their heavy borrowings, the companies can be vulnerable to interest rate rises.

Property Companies

Some investors may still not feel comfortable with taking the plunge straight into commercial property. An alternative is to invest, via the stock market, in the shares of property development companies. Returns can be high. In fact, some property developers have done extremely well. Examples are Westfield Holdings, which develops and manages many of the shopping centres owned by Westfield Trust, and Lend Lease, which has involvements in commercial property developments in several countries.

However, they can also be volatile. It is important to understand that these are stock market investments, not property investments. Residential property developers, in particular, have shown great volatility, in line with the housing cycle. But having said that, Westfield Holdings has been one of the all-time stand-out investments of the Australian Stock Exchange. According to the company's 2000 annual report: 'An investment of $1,000 in Westfield shares when they listed in 1960 was worth approximately $109 million at 30 June 2000.'

Summary

Investors wanting exposure to commercial property have many options, in addition to the purchase of direct property or of units in a listed property trust. In this chapter we have covered:

1. property securities funds

2. unlisted property trusts

3. mortgage trusts

4. mezzanine finance

5. infrastructure investments

6. property companies.

Commercial Property Investment Performance Index

Since 1985, the Property Council of Australia has been compiling an index of returns from commercial property, based on income and capital gain. At the end of 2002, the index was based on 593 properties valued at nearly $45 billion. These figures show annual return—that is, income and capital gain, minus expenses—as a percentage of the value of the property.

Table 1: Commercial Property Investment Performance Index

YEAR ENDING	OFFICE	RETAIL	INDUSTRIAL
Dec-85	17.0%	17.0%	12.8%
Jun-86	16.6%	14.2%	14.0%
Dec-86	18.1%	14.8%	17.1%
Jun-87	20.5%	18.7%	16.1%

Year Ending	Office	Retail	Industrial
Dec-87	26.4%	24.6%	19.1%
Jun-88	35.2%	25.5%	23.1%
Dec-88	34.2%	28.4%	23.4%
Jun-89	25.3%	24.7%	21.2%
Dec-89	16.0%	15.3%	18.2%
Jun-90	10.5%	14.1%	10.6%
Dec-90	0.2%	12.7%	-0.6%
Jun-91	-10.6%	9.2%	-6.4%
Dec-91	-13.6%	6.9%	-9.9%
Jun-92	-13.5%	9.0%	-5.9%
Dec-92	-12.6%	10.9%	2.7%
Jun-93	-11.3%	11.9%	0.3%
Dec-93	-6.6%	12.1%	2.7%
Jun-94	5.5%	14.2%	12.5%
Dec-94	11.6%	14.1%	16.5%
Jun-95	9.7%	10.7%	15.4%
Dec-95	7.1%	9.4%	14.7%
Jun-96	6.7%	8.7%	14.2%
Dec-96	7.2%	8.2%	13.1%
Jun-97	8.4%	8.4%	15.1%
Dec-97	10.8%	8.7%	16.1%
Jun-98	10.5%	9.7%	15.1%

YEAR ENDING	OFFICE	RETAIL	INDUSTRIAL
Dec-98	9.9%	9.9%	15.0%
Jun-99	8.9%	11.1%	14.6%
Dec-99	8.5%	10.7%	13.4%
Jun-00	10.0%	11.5%	12.2%
Dec-00	11.0%	12.7%	12.2%
Jun-01	11.0%	11.2%	12.5%
Dec-01	10.0%	10.3%	12.4%
Jun-02	8.6%	10.7%	11.6%
Dec-02	8.0%	11.7%	12.6%

(Figures show annual return—that is, income and capital gain, minus expenses—as a percentage of the value of the property.)

Source: © Property Council of Australia—Investment Performance Index. Reproduced with permission.

Your Resource Centre

This book is intended to serve as a comprehensive introduction to commercial property investment. We believe that it can set you well on the path to success.

But continuing your education is crucial, if you are truly to become a successful investor. The property market is always changing. An investment that is right to buy one year might be one where you've missed the boat were you to buy it several years later.

Unfortunately, in stark comparison to the stock market or residential property investment, there is a lack of data on commercial property.

Many professionals and advisers do not want to divulge the information that investors—beginners particularly—truly need. They seem to consider it 'secret agents' business', which they feel ought not to be disclosed to the general public, or at least not free of charge. The result is that their publicity material and websites are little more than glossy corporate brochures—sometimes more fluff than substance.

Nevertheless, there are some organisations and companies giving out generous amounts of comprehensive and regularly updated information, particularly on the internet. The wise investor will bookmark these sites and return to them regularly.

You'll find the internet to be an ever-changing banquet. Excellent new sites will certainly emerge. Others—once excellent—may become obsolete, frozen in cyber-time with misleading and out-of-date information.

Three Websites You Should Visit Often

The following three websites are particularly generous in both the quantity and quality of information that they offer.

Property Council of Australia

Website: www.propertyoz.com.au

This, the mother of all commercial property websites, contains a huge amount of data. A highlight is the book *Build Your Wealth*, an introduction to the principles of commercial property investment, which can be downloaded free (click on the Bookshop link).

The 'CyberStats' section is, in the site's own words:

> ...a free online information resource bursting with up-to-the minute property and economic data. CyberStats contains more than 100 economic indicators critical to the prosperity of international and domestic property markets.

The 'Brain Snax' section is a database of several hundred articles on the commercial property market, from myriad sources. Titles range from 'New Investment Frontiers—Reshaping Hotel Investment' and 'Features of the Office Property Market' to 'Managing Shopping Centre Tenant Mix' and 'Changes in the Commercial Real Estate Industry'.

The Council publishes the monthly *Property Australia* journal, and selected articles are placed on the site.

Other resources include a bookshop, information about commercial property training courses, a property search function and numerous links.

Property Investment Research

Website: www.pir.com.au

Property Investment Research is one of Australia's leading independent research firms in the field of commercial property. Its published material is expensive (though often discounted for individual investors), and is aimed particularly at finance and property professionals. However, its website contains much useful introductory material, particularly for those looking to buy into managed investments.

An investments section presents guidance on choosing an appropriate commercial property investment. There is an extensive section on listed property trusts, including a glossary and a list of frequently asked questions. Also on the site is an overview of the property syndication market, and a media section with articles about property.

In addition, full details are available of PIR's many publications.

Gardner+Lang

Website: www.gal.com.au

Co-author Chris Lang is Managing Director of property consultants Gardner+Lang, and is responsible for this most comprehensive and well-organised website.

The site offers, free of charge to all visitors, a complete training course in commercial property fundamentals, along with monthly eBulletins that provide further instruction, plus up-to-date market trends and opportunities.

An extensive archive section will provide you with answers to numerous investor queries. Other highlights include the interactive property rating matrix, a wide-ranging section on property syndication and case studies of successful property investments.

Some More Useful Websites

Here are some more useful sites:

- ➲ Property managers SAITeysMcMahon have created an excellent website (www.saiteysmcmahon.com) with a considerable amount of educational material, including a section on investing basics, and a glossary.

- ➲ The Australian Direct Property Investment Association (www.adpia.com.au) website contains a lot of data on the performance of commercial property investment. It also offers for download a 12-page introduction to property syndicates.

- ➲ Australian PropertyWeb (www.propertyweb.com.au) is mainly a comprehensive listing of commercial and residential properties for sale and lease. However, it also maintains an extensive series of commercial real estate links, and its Research page contains some property market and economic statistics.

➲ Real Estate Australia (www.realestate.com.au) is another large listings service. It also contains a large selection of articles on real estate buying (aimed mainly at residential property purchasers, but with application for commercial property), along with numerous calculators, a frequently asked questions section and a real estate glossary.

➲ Property Look (www.propertylook.com.au) and property.com.au (www.property.com.au) are other large listing portals, with useful collections of links.

➲ Commercial Price Guide (www.commercialpriceguide.com.au) from Australian Property Monitors is an online service that provides details of prices paid for commercial property in selected areas.

➲ ANZ Banking publishes, twice a year, a 12-page *Property Outlook*, covering commercial and residential property. It is available, along with other economic commentaries, at the bank's website (www.anz.com.au).

➲ Accounting and management consulting giant Ernst & Young operates a Real Estate Advisory Services team with occasional research publications available (www.ey.com.au).

➲ BIS Shrapnel is one of Australia's leading economic forecasters. It issues regular reports on commercial property, and though these are for subscribers only, summaries of many of them are available at its website (www.bis.com.au).

Real Estate Companies

Most companies involved in real estate now maintain their own websites. As already noted, these are often little more than the equivalent of glossy corporate brochures (and sometimes not even that), with little actual substance. But some are reasonably generous in publishing on their sites research reports, articles and newsletters.

We have found useful material at the following:

- CB Richard Ellis (www.cbrichardellis.com.au)
- Charter Keck Cramer (www.charterkc.com.au)
- Colliers International (www.colliers.com/australia/)
- Fitzroys (www.fitzroys.com.au)
- Herron Todd White (www.htw.com.au)
- Knight Frank (www.knightfrank.com.au)
- Jones Lang LaSalle (www.joneslanglasalle.com.au)
- McGees (www.mcgees.com.au)
- Quartile Property Network (www.quartile.com.au).

Public Property Syndicates

Most property companies offering syndicates have websites, often with data about new investments and reports for earlier offerings. For those new to this field, it can be worthwhile reading the syndicate prospectuses that are sometimes on these sites:

- Austgrowth Property Syndicates (www.austgrowth.com.au) is worth visiting for a lengthy collection of newspaper articles explaining the syndication process. And MCS

Property (www.mcsproperty.com.au) presents some
information on property investment. (MCS Property
has been acquired by Centro Properties Group.
However, the MCS website was still functioning in
mid-2003 when this book was written.)

➲ A firm of solicitors, McMahon Clarke Legal
(www.mcmahonclarke.com) publishes an occasional
e-newsletter *Syndicate News*, which is available at the
website, along with papers on the subject that have been
prepared for various conferences. Partner Greg
McMahon has written the book *Everything You Need to
Know about Property Syndication*, and this can be ordered
via the website.

➲ Another firm of solicitors, MDRN Group
(www.mdrn.com.au), has prepared some articles on
syndicates.

➲ Lonsdale Securities has on its website a lot of samples of
its research into property syndicates (www.lonsec.com.au).

Other syndicate managers include the following:

➲ Abacus Property Group (www.abacusproperty.com.au)

➲ Australian Unity (www.australianunity.com.au)

➲ Centro Property Syndicates (www.syndicates.centro.com.au)

➲ Challenger International (www.challengergroup.com.au)

➲ Cromwell Corporation (www.cromwell.com.au)

➲ DB Real Estate (www.realestate.australia.db.com)

➲ Domaine Property Funds (www.domaineproperty.com)

➲ Elderslie Group (www.efc.com.au)

- ➲ Glenmont Properties (www.glenmont.com.au)

- ➲ Investa Property Group (www.investa.com.au)

- ➲ Macquarie Direct Property (www.macquarie.com.au/au/property/direct/)

- ➲ Westpoint Corporation (www.westpoint.com.au).

Listed Property Trusts

You will find a huge amount of research is published regularly on the listed property trusts sector of the stock market, and most stockbrokers have reports available. Magazines like *Shares* and *Personal Investor*, along with the finance sections of many newspapers, also often feature articles on this topic.

The Australian Stock Exchange website (www.asx.com.au) carries an extensive amount of introductory data in its Managed Investments section, as well as performance tables, charts, media articles and a collection of links, including to the websites of most of the trusts.

The business and accountancy consulting firm BDO Kendalls prepares an annual Listed Property Trust Survey. The 92-page 2003 edition is available on its website (www.bdokendalls.com.au).

The websites of listed property trust managers often include extensive details of properties held by the trusts, along with unit prices, annual reports and stock exchange announcements.

Major funds management and property securities groups include:

- ➲ Abacus Property Group (www.abacusproperty.com.au)

- ➲ AMP (www.amp.com.au)

- APN Funds Management (www.apngroup.com.au)

- Australian Growth Properties (www.363george.com.au)

- Bunnings Warehouse Property Trust
  (www.bunningspropertytrust.com.au)

- Centro Properties Group (www.centro.com.au)

- Colonial First State (www.colonialfirststate.com.au)

- DB Real Estate (www.realestate.australia.db.com)

- Deutsche Asset Management (www.am.australia.db.com)

- Gandel Retail Management (www.gandel.com.au)

- General Property Trust (www.gpt.com.au)

- ING Real Estate (www.ingrealestate.com.au)

- Investa Property Group (www.investa.com.au)

- Ipoh (www.ipoh.com.au)

- James Fielding Group (www.jamesfielding.com.au)

- Lend Lease Corporation (www.lendlease.com.au)

- Macquarie Property Trusts (www.macquarie.com.au/au/
  business/property_trusts/overview.htm)

- Mirvac Group (www.mirvac.com.au)

- MLC (www.mlc.com.au)

- Principal Financial Group (www.principalglobal.com/
  australia/)

- Stockland Trust Group (www.stockland.com.au)

- Thakral Holdings Group (www.thakral.com.au)

- ⮑ Tyndall (www.tyndall.com.au)

- ⮑ Valad Property Group (www.valad.com.au)

- ⮑ Westfield Trust (www.westfield.com.au)

- ⮑ Westpac Banking (www.westpac.com.au).

Banks

The banks were amongst the earliest Australian companies to embrace the potential of the internet, and today many of them maintain huge, sprawling websites with enormous amounts of information. For the commercial property investor this might include economic reports and even commentaries on the property market, details of property financing schemes and information on property-related managed trusts.

The main bank sites are:

- ⮑ Adelaide Bank (www.adelaidebank.com.au)

- ⮑ ANZ (www.anz.com.au)

- ⮑ Bank of Queensland (www.boq.com.au)

- ⮑ Bank of Western Australia (www.bankwest.com.au)

- ⮑ Bendigo Bank (www.bendigobank.com.au)

- ⮑ Citibank Australia (www.citibank.com.au)

- ⮑ Commonwealth Bank (www.commbank.com.au)

- ⮑ Macquarie Bank (www.macquarie.com.au)

- ⮑ National Australia Bank (www.national.com.au)

- ⮑ St George Bank (www.stgeorge.com.au)

➲ Suncorp-Metway (www.suncorp.com.au)

➲ Westpac Banking (www.westpac.com.au).

Infochoice.com.au (www.infochoice.com.au) and Cannex (www.cannex.com.au) are websites with a lot of comparative information on banking products.

Investor Websites

Most investor websites are mainly concerned with the stock market, and to a lesser extent with residential property investments. However, you can sometimes find useful articles on commercial property.

Money Manager (www.moneymanager.com.au) is part of the Fairfax media group, and reproduces selected investor articles from the group's newspapers and magazines.

The NineMSN web portal incorporates a finance section (ninemsn.com.au/finance/) with substantial amounts of investor information, including a property section.

Exchanges

The Australian Stock Exchange (www.asx.com.au) contains a huge amount of information relating to stock market investments, including, as already noted, on listed property trusts.

The Bendigo Stock Exchange (www.bsx.com.au) provides a modest amount of trading data on a small number of property trusts and syndicates. Austock Brokers (www.austock.com.au) presents some data on its Exempt Property Market.

Professional Organisations

The websites of professional bodies are sometimes useful sources of statistical data and other information. The Property Council of Australia has already been cited for maintaining one of the best commercial property websites.

The Real Estate Institute of Australia (www.reiaustralia.com.au) site, though concerned primarily with residential property, has a useful section on the costs involved in real estate purchases, and a comprehensive collection of links.

A couple of others are:

➲ Australian Property Institute
(www.propertyinstitute.com.au)

➲ Shopping Centre Council of Australia
(www.propertyoz.com.au/retail/).

The Australian Securities and Investments Commission's very comprehensive website (www.asic.gov.au) is particularly concerned with educating investors on potential scams. For example, it advises investors in real estate to:

➲ Be wary of pressure selling techniques.

➲ Make sure your decision fits into your overall investment strategy.

➲ Understand the risks involved.

➲ Decide whether you need professional advice.

➲ Decide whether to invest directly or indirectly.

➲ Do your homework.

➲ Learn about borrowing money to invest.

➲ Consider the tax and social security implications.

Advisory papers on the site include:

➲ Investing in real estate.

➲ Scams and dodgy seminars.

➲ Mortgage lending schemes offering sky-high returns.

➲ Protect your money from 'get rich quick' pushers.

➲ Offshore investment seminars.

➲ Inside an investment seminar—a true story.

➲ Read our warnings about psychologically charged seminars.

➲ Mezzanine investing and the two golden rules.

➲ Seven tips for choosing a managed investment scheme.

➲ Borrowing to invest.

➲ Choosing a financial adviser.

Other Government Websites

Some government websites offer information of direct (or indirect) relevance to property investors. The best starting point is the Australian Government Information web portal (www.nla.gov.au/oz/gov/), which is run by the National Library of Australia, and which maintains links to federal and state government organs.

fed.gov.au (www.fed.gov.au) is the official federal government entry portal to all its websites.

Several other useful sites are:

➲ Australian Bureau of Statistics (www.abs.gov.au)

➲ Australian Taxation Office (www.ato.gov.au)

➲ Commonwealth Treasury (www.treasury.gov.au).

Publications

➲ *The Australian* (www.theaustralian.com.au) is less comprehensive than *The Australian Financial Review*, though its 'Prime Space' commercial property supplement, in the paper each Thursday, provides some excellent features on the sector.

➲ *The Australian Financial Review* carries regular coverage of commercial property developments. Most of its website (www.afr.com.au) is for subscribers only, but some bits are for any visitor.

➲ *The Australian Property Investor* journal, covers mainly residential property, though also has some articles on the commercial property sector. Information about the magazine is available at its website (www.apimagazine.com.au).

➲ *The Australian Property Journal* is published quarterly by the Australian Property Institute. Its articles are aimed mainly at those in the profession, but are sometimes of interest to the investor. Details are at the Institute's website (www.propertyinstitute.com.au).

➲ *Money* magazine also publishes some articles on property, and maintains a file of these at its website (finance.ninemsn.com.au/money/).

➲ *Personal Investor* (www.personalinvestor.com.au) and *BRW* (www.brw.com.au) magazines both sometimes publish articles on commercial property investment, and these are at the websites for subscribers.

➲ *Property Australia* is a monthly journal published by the Property Council of Australia. Details, and selected articles, are at the Council's website (www.propertyoz.com.au).

➲ *Your Mortgage* magazine carries, as the name implies, extensive data on bank lending. Its website (www.yourmortgage.com.au) includes an extensive collection of links to mortgage providers and related institutions.

➲ Two locally published books by the prolific Nick Renton, *Understanding Investment Property* and *Learn More About Property*, contain information on commercial property investing.

How to Negotiate Your Way to Success

Here are some tips that might help you in your negotiations.

Agendas

If you are a novice negotiator, you might automatically assume that the items listed on your agenda would be identical to those on the other person's agenda. So this might come as a surprise to you: in all Gardner+Lang's negotiations since 1970, we've never found our clients' agendas to be the same as the other parties'. There may have been one or two similar items on both lists, but their order of priority was always different.

The secret is, try to establish what is on their agenda, and in what order. And you can often simply do this before the negotiation process 'formally' begins—just through observation, or by asking questions, and then listening carefully.

Bold Statements

If you ever make a bold statement, always be prepared to back up (or act upon) whatever you say. Otherwise, you have left yourself with nowhere to go.

Competition

Whenever you can, try to create the illusion of having options, and your proposition suddenly appears a lot more attractive. The power of competition is what increases the value of whatever you're offering.

Deadlines

Most deadlines are artificial and, therefore, flexible. You will soon discover that stated deadlines tend to be set through some form of negotiation in the first place. Therefore, you'll generally find them to be negotiable as they start to loom closer.

Expertise

Perception tends to become reality—but it's not necessarily the truth. You see, by carefully establishing your credentials and experience during the very early stages of a negotiation, you can often cause the other side to allow many of your later statements go unchallenged.

Facade

Have you ever been kept waiting for meetings, or been treated in an offhand manner, during a negotiation? There are people who will display a scant regard for timetables, or even for doing the deal, as a clever ploy to convince you that they really don't care.

218

Greed

Don't get 'bent out of shape' when sellers are wanting too much. If they insist on naming the price, you just focus upon naming the terms. You will often end up with the better deal.

Halt

More often than not, you will find the deal improves whenever you are prepared to walk away from the table.

Investment

When you discover more about 'method' and 'ultimatums' later, you'll appreciate just how important the power of investment really is. The more time, energy and money you can cause someone to invest the more likely they are to modify their position, as the negotiation process draws to a close.

Jackpot

Whenever a deal looks too good to be true, it probably is. Never allow yourself to become mesmerised by the people, the surroundings, or the price. Just stick to the fundamentals.

Knowledge

If you possess superior knowledge about any particular transaction, then you hold a competitive edge throughout the negotiating process. This includes your knowledge about the market, the locality, the property, the other party and their specific needs. However, unless you have the time to collate all that knowledge for yourself, you may be far better off retaining someone who can—someone who'll act exclusively on your behalf.

Legitimacy

It is difficult to argue against the power of the printed word. Think about it: signs tend to govern your life, every day. Do you actually challenge them? Probably not. However, that doesn't mean you can't start to from now on.

If you're selling, you can use that to your advantage—because very few people will challenge the standard wording on a printed contract. Just place it before them, and simply wait for them to make the next move. The only reason they may appear to be 'reading' it is to justify the commitment they're about to make.

Method

You have basically two choices as to which style you'll adopt during the negotiation process—an open (collaborative) style, or a closed (combative) style. And they are not necessarily mutually exclusive. If you start by being open and friendly, you will generally be able to build up an early trust. On the other hand, if you find the other party is closed and aggressive, you can quickly change your style.

However, if you start off aggressively, then you may find it hard to adopt a friendly, open approach later without losing a great deal of credibility. Try to position yourself as a firm, but reasonable, negotiator.

Numbers

Somehow, round numbers tend to come across as being negotiable. On the other hand, 'odd' numbers always appear much firmer. They appear to convey the impression that you have spent a considerable amount of time and effort in formulating them.

Objections

Human nature being what it is, people need to say 'No!' But they are often merely making a response, and not actually taking a position, when they do so. Mostly, they are simply conveying: 'You haven't given me enough information yet for me to reach the decision you're asking me to make.'

Persistence

Sometimes, when all else fails, persistence is the only thing that will win through for you. You'll be surprised how many people will throw up countless objections, simply to see if you've got what it takes. Napoleon Hill seemed to sum it up well, when he said: 'Effort only fully releases its reward, after a person refuses to quit.'

Questions

Learn to ask questions, even when you think you might know the answers. Whenever you're prepared to ask for help, you start to establish a climate of trust. And if you're asking the questions you'll tend to control the negotiation. Sometimes you can even answer a question, by asking a further question of your own in response—simply to regain the initiative. And, if you don't like their response, just reply to them with: 'Tell me, why are you saying that?'

You achieve two things by doing this: firstly, you buy yourself some 'thinking time', and secondly, you force them to better justify their stated position.

Reactions

Whenever you make an emotional outburst, you tend to give up some control. It might be okay for you to act in anger, but never allow yourself to react that way.

221

Silence

'Top talkers' (as opposed to top salespeople) will generally feel awkward, after even the slightest pause. And, more often than not, they will start to improve on their stated position for you. Whenever you ask a 'closing question', simply pause. And just wait patiently for them to speak—even if it takes them several minutes to do so.

Sometimes, the silence will be deafening. But invariably, this single tactic will bring you more success than anything else. And you'll soon learn to appreciate the joy of silence. Once you have reached agreement, always make sure you change the subject and move on to the documentation, straight away, before they start having any second thoughts.

Timing

Sometimes you will fail—not because your proposition was bad or your execution was poor, but simply because your timing wasn't right. Don't abandon your idea; be prepared to reintroduce it again at a later (more appropriate) time.

Ultimatums

You can only really expect your ultimatum to work if you have allowed the other party to invest a considerable amount of time, energy and money into the negotiation. Therefore, ultimatums tend to work best at the end, not the beginning, of the negotiation process. And it's always best to offer them a choice. That way they view your position as being 'Which alternative do you prefer?', rather than 'Take it, or leave it!'

Venturesome

You can often try changing tactics, in order to search out a weakness. And then, listen very carefully to what is actually being said. Even be prepared to enter into 'minor skirmishes', as you attempt to gain concessions.

Weakness

In any negotiation, when you appear to know everything, that's the quickest way to get the other party offside. It's better for you to appear slightly naive, rather than overly knowledgeable; dumb, rather than smart. In fact, it can be to your advantage to say, 'I'm not sure that I quite understand.' Or, 'Could you please explain that to me once more?'

Nothing disarms the other party's logic and arguments more easily than having to deal with someone like that. It renders their attempts at persuading you virtually worthless.

X

In years gone by, when you asked some people to sign a document, they often did so by handwriting an 'X' onto the page. But, here's a quick word of advice: Never, ever ask the other side to 'sign' anything! You see, most people have been told: 'Don't sign any documents, before you consult your lawyer.' Even knowing that, you'll find the very same people seem quite prepared to okay it, confirm it, acknowledge it, and (even) approve it.

And yet, they probably started the negotiation process with the intention of signing nothing!

So, isn't it interesting what you can achieve, simply through your choice of words?

Yardstick

You'll invariably find that trust will build throughout a negotiation as you are seen as being trustworthy when it comes to the promises, or undertakings you may give, along the way. It's important that you are seen as being consistent during each negotiation. But don't allow yourself to become predictable, from one negotiation to another.

Zest

You should approach negotiating as a game—albeit, a very serious game.

You do need to care; but not that much. Because, as soon as you simply must have something, it will end up costing you far too much.

Property Trust
Performance

On the following three pages is a table from the Australian Stock Exchange website (from August 2003) showing the performance of listed property trusts.

Property Trusts

ASX Code	Name	Size (mil)	Prices $		Returns %		
			Year high	Year low	1yr	3yr	5 yr
ABP	Abacus Property	329	1.25	1.08	n/a	n/a	n/a
ADP	AMP Diversified	1597	3.19	2.48	24.78	18.22	12.95
AIP	AMP Industrial Trust	416	1.28	1.04	12.05	13.84	12.0
AOF	AMP Office Trust	1032	1.26	1.06	1.83	7.03	7.02
ART	AMP Shopping Centre	1403	1.83	1.33	25.75	16.17	n/a
AGH	Australian Growth Properties	262	0.90	0.65	16.27	29.16	15.44
AHO	Australian Hotel	17	0.47	0.30	0.34	-18.4	-13.7
BWP	Bunnings Warehouse	402	1.70	1.27	22.5	23.86	n/a
CDP	Carindale Property	182	2.64	2.21	16.7	20.1	n/a
CEP	Centro Properties	2193	4.29	3.50	18.67	21.62	19.06
GAN	CFS Gandel Retail Trust	2440	1.48	1.17	12.87	13.98	10.64
CPA	Commonwealth Property	1735	1.32	1.11	8.09	16.71	n/a
CNR	Coonawarra	11	0.96	0.55	n/a	n/a	n/a
DDF	Deutsche Diversified	1094	1.27	1.05	2.24	8.54	5.48
DIT	Deutsche Industrial	594	1.89	1.55	10.79	16.97	13.58
DOT	Deutsche Office	1286	1.30	1.05	-10.19	1.32	n/a
FPF	Flexi Property Fund	75	1.24	1.12	10.49	21.39	13.86
GPT	General Property Trust	5693	3.16	2.70	11.63	10.44	9.8
GST	GPT Split Trust	65	2.66	2.32	10.39	8.98	8.7

226

ASX Code	Name	Size (mil)	Prices $		Returns %		
			Year high	Year low	1yr	3yr	5 yr
GHG	Grand Hotel Group	104	0.68	0.46	-16.1	-18.4	-14.5
IYS	Infrastructure Yield Securities	44	1.45	1.00	-21.4	n/a	n/a
IIF	ING Industrial Fund	1111	1.87	1.61	14.44	14.73	14.29
IOF	ING Office Fund	937	1.25	1.10	3.8	9.34	n/a
IPG	Investa Property	1753	2.24	1.92	5.03	14.38	11.88
JFG	James Fielding	341	3.37	2.87	15.82	n/a	n/a
JFM	JF Meridian Trust	415	1.17	1.00	23.29	23.4	16.33
KIT	Kiwi Income Property Trust	441	n/a	n/a	n/a	n/a	n/a
LUO	Lend Lease US Office	773	1.58	1.20	3.66	n/a	n/a
MCW	Macquarie Countrywide	883	1.87	1.53	14.91	14.28	12.98
MGI	Macquarie Goodman	1692	1.64	1.38	13.8	17.44	14.44
MLE	Macquarie Leisure	113	0.81	0.78	31.46	10.48	n/a
MOF	Macquarie Office	1031	1.34	1.13	-3.19	3.46	9.88
MORPA	Macquarie Park Street	97	109.0	98.50	12.8	n/a	n/a
MPR	Macquarie Prologis	661	1.26	1.00	55.0	n/a	n/a
MPY	MFS Hotel Property	1	0.15	0.04	-15.1	-47.7	n/a
MGR	Mirvac Group	2991	4.80	3.97	13.67	17.2	n/a
MME	MTM Entertainment	27	0.27	0.12	38.88	7.72	n/a
PPB	Pelorus PIPES	24	4.00	3.16	n/a	n/a	n/a
PRX	Prime Retail Group	204	1.04	0.91	13.62	28.12	14.05
POF	Principal Office Fund	1436	1.69	1.25	10.52	10.95	8.75
RRT	Record Realty	37	0.96	0.85	n/a	n/a	n/a

ASX Code	Name	Size (mil)	Prices $		Returns %		
			Year high	Year low	1yr	3yr	5 yr
SGP	Stockland Trust Group	4690	5.50	4.18	17.85	19.13	13.91
THG	Thakral Holdings	350	0.70	0.57	-0.83	12.26	9.93
TLT	Tourism & Leisure	9	0.65	0.30	102.48	55.13	-6.74
VPG	Valad Property	241	1.05	0.89	n/a	n/a	n/a
WFA	Westfield America	7297	2.23	1.91	12.1	17.86	15.14
WFT	Westfield Trust	7432	3.67	3.21	8.79	9.5	9.2
WST	Westralia Property Trust	16	1.05	0.80	n/a	n/a	n/a

Source: © Australian Stock Exchange Limited.
Reproduced with permission.

Glossary

Helping You Understand Property Jargon

Agent: the person or firm appointed in writing by you to act on your behalf with third parties, and thereby receive a commission.

Agents in conjunction: you (as a vendor or landlord) may appoint more than one agent, or an appointed agent may act with another agent who introduces a purchaser or tenant to your property.

Air rights: rights concerning the building upon, or occupancy of, the vertical space above the specified site.

Allotment: a small site for home building, sometimes called a block.

Amortisation: regular repayments are made over an agreed time to recover your capital investment.

Anchor tenant: the big-name tenant in a shopping complex, often a major supermarket or department store, which attracts other tenants and customers.

Apartment: originally, the American word for a flat, but in Australia it might also be a suite or just a room, not necessarily self-contained.

Appreciation: an increase in property values triggered by inflation, improvements or increased demand.

Arcade: a covered walkway, usually with shops along both sides.

Arrears: debts, usually rents, which have not been paid on time.

Assessment: the rates or taxes apportioned to a particular property.

Assets: the sum of a person's real and personal property, including equities.

Assignment: the transfer of a property, a lease, rights or an interest and sometimes a liability from one party to another.

Average: the term is Subject to Average and it is used by insurers when responding to a claim on property which has been covered for less than its full value.

Body Corporate: the legal administrative group of owners of offices, home units, flats, town houses, etc. for common property.

Bona fide: genuine, honest, in good faith.

Bridging finance: a temporary loan to bridge the time gap between paying for one property and receiving payment from a previous property.

Building line: the uniform distance, usually from a road, behind which buildings must be erected.

Building regulations: laws laying down standards in materials and construction methods which you must observe to maintain health, safety and certain design minimums in any building or alteration.

Buying commission: the money you pay to an agent for helping you to acquire a specific type of building.

Capital gain: the profitable difference between your buying price and selling price, now subject to capital gains tax.

Capital improved value: the amount of money a property might reasonably be expected to realise if sold at the time of a municipal valuation.

Cashflow: the surplus income, usually charted monthly, flowing into a property investment or business after servicing and operating costs have been deducted.

Caveat emptor: let the buyer beware.

Central Business District (CBD): the designated downtown business area for a major city.

Certificate of Title: the paper that records property ownership. One copy is lodged at the Titles Office and the other with the proprietor. When the property is sold, the Titles Office annotates both copies.

Client: a person who engages an agent or valuer, and who is obliged to pay that agent or valuer a commission or fees.

Commercial property: for business purposes, office buildings, shops, warehouses, hotels, etc.

Compensation: the money paid to a property owner when all or part of the property is compulsorily acquired by a statutory authority. It takes into account such things as market value, the effect on the balance of the property and loss of income.

Compound interest: the combination of interest paid on the principal and on interest accrued.

Condominium: an American term starting to come into Australian usage covering ownership of a flat or unit and the owner's interest in parts of the property used by other owners.

Consideration: the price.

Consolidation of title: when several parcels of land are put together, a new Certificate of Title is issued to replace all the earlier certificates.

Construction costs: the sum of labour and material costs, plus contractors' overheads and profits in the erection or improvement of a property.

Corridor development: planning schemes calling for 'finger development' of urban dwellings with rural land in between.

Counterpart: an identical copy of an original document.

Covenant: an agreement between landlord and tenant, or vendor and purchaser, covering specific things which will be done or cannot be done to a property.

Cover note: immediate insurance cover, often issued by an insurance broker on the insurance company's behalf, for a property which has just been bought.

Date of settlement: the day, under the terms of the contract, when a vendor is obliged to transfer a property to the purchaser.

Deferred income: future income as from a lease which included periodic rent increases.

Depreciation: drop in a property's value due to passage of time, deterioration, or changes to neighbouring properties.

Also: book depreciation is the amount you can claim for tax purposes for the replacement of an asset.

Developer: a person who buys property and by improving it—through sub-division or construction, for instance—lifts its value.

Direct costs: site costs (purchase price plus legal expenses plus commission), plus improvement cost (plans and permits plus professional fees plus construction).

District business centre: the heart of a substantial shopping centre in a suburb.

Easement: the contractual right of one person to use a portion of another person's land, usually as a drive for access or as a run-off for water.

Economic life: the potential number of years a property could be profitable.

Effective rate: the real rate of return or repayment, as opposed to the nominal rate.

Environmental impact study: an expert's assessment of the long-term environmental effects of a particular land-use scheme.

Equity: the percentage of a property an owner holds after outstanding loans have been deducted from the market value.

Essential services: statutorily monitored services within a property—including air conditioning, fire services, lifts and electrical equipment—which will attract significant fines for you, as the owner, for noncompliance.

Facade: the front face of a building.

Foreclosure: the legal action to possess a property, which a mortgagee takes when a mortgagor defaults on payments.

Freehold: a property which is owned outright and for unlimited duration.

General law title: such a title pre-dates the Torrens Title System under which ownership is government-recorded by Certificates of Title; it is based on a comprehensive history of ownership.

Head room: the distance from floor to ceiling.

Heavy industry: a zoning term covering noisy, smelly or otherwise unattractive industries.

Hectare: the metric measurement of land area equal to 10,000 square metres, or 2.47 acres.

Height density: another zoning regulation limiting the height of buildings in a particular area.

High rise: a building over three or four storeys, usually requiring a lift. It is an indefinite term. In offices, generally a building over 30 storeys.

Home units: individually owned homes in a development of two or more homes, usually owner-occupied rather than rented.

Industrial park: a considerable development over a large area, tailored to the requirements—water, roads, landscaping, etc.—of industry.

Insurable interest: as soon as you sign a contract to buy a property, you have an insurable interest and are wise to cover it.

Interest-only loan: the borrower is obliged to pay interest over the term of the loan but not to amortise the principal, repaying it in a lump sum at the end.

Interim development order: enables a planning authority to control development of an area before the final scheme is gazetted.

Investment return: the rate per month (or year) of return on an investment, produced by rental and/or resale.

Irrevocable: cannot be undone.

Joint venture: where two or more people or companies combine to carry out a project or enterprise.

Land usage: determined by zoning regulations—residential, industrial, etc.

Landlord: the owner of a property for leasing.

Lease: the formal arrangement by which one party has use of another's property in return for rent.

Lease with option to purchase: a lease embodying the right of the lessee to buy the property at an agreed price within an agreed time.

Lessor: the party who grants a lease.

Leverage: putting into a property a low amount of capital and borrowing the balance to achieve the best return on your capital.

Maintenance: the expenditure required to keep a property in an efficient operating condition.

Managing agent: a real estate agent authorised by you to manage your property.

Market price: the price paid for a property: it is real, whereas 'market value' is only an estimate.

Mezzanine: an intermediary floor, usually between the ground and first floors.

Mezzanine finance: a high-yielding investment in property development, filling the gap between bank lending and the developer's own equity, and sometimes with a second mortgage over the property.

Mortgage: a document pledging a property as security for the repayment of the money you borrow on the property.

Mortgage fund: a managed fund that invests in mortgages.

Mortgagee: the lender on the mortgage.

Mortgagee in possession: the mortgagee gets a court order to take possession of the property, usually after a mortgagor defaults.

Mortgagor: the borrower.

Net lease: where your lessee is responsible for all building outgoings on top of the agreed rent.

Notice to Quit: enables, under strict conditions, a landlord or tenant to terminate a tenancy without the agreement of the other.

Option: in selling, the right (secured by a payment) to purchase a property at an agreed price on or before an agreed date. In leases, the right to renew at a mutually agreed rent.

Outgoings: all expenses on a property.

Own-your-own flats: the expanding practice of people buying, rather than renting, flats and units. Usually the owner gets a separate title and undertakes to pay a proper proportion of running costs for the whole building.

Parking ratio: the ratio of parking places to office area or number of flats—a very important consideration these days.

Passed in: when a property fails at auction to reach the vendor's reserve price. (The highest bidder has the right to meet the reserve price or try to negotiate an acceptable price.)

Peppercorn rent: historically, a rent of one peppercorn a year; in fact a method by which a landlord can let a property for virtually nothing, but retain all ownership rights.

Plot ratio: the ratio of building area to site area.

Property management: a real estate agent manages properties for landlords, ensuring the property complies with legislation and regulations at all times, and is also responsible for selecting tenants, collecting rents, arranging maintenance and so on.

Property securities fund: a managed fund which owns units in a variety of listed property trusts, and sometimes also in other property assets.

Property syndicate: a group that is formed, under a legal structure, to invest in a property asset for a specific term. Large public syndicates are run by property management companies.

Property trust: a managed investment in property. Most trusts are listed on the Australian Stock Exchange.

Property wealth: the difference between the market value of your properties and the amount of money you owe on them.

Public liability: the insurance taken by companies and private individuals to protect themselves against claims made by members of the public who might be injured in some way on the property.

Quantity surveyor: a professional who calculates the materials required for a construction, and also helps you to compile your depreciation schedule.

Rateable value: the estimated value of a property on which rates are assessed.

Real property: the ownership of physical real estate land and buildings.

Redevelopment: the updating of urban property, usually by demolition and rebuilding.

Regional shopping centre: a drive-in development with department stores, supermarkets and specialty shops which are replacing the ribbons of shops along both sides of busy streets.

Reserve price: the lowest price at which a vendor is prepared to sell a property at auction.

Restrictive covenant: land is sold with, perhaps, the covenant that only one home can be built upon it or that the home must be built at a specified cost or height.

Rezoning: a planning term in which the local authority can alter a planning scheme to allow, say, commercial rather than residential building.

Sale and lease back: an investor buys a property and leases it back to the seller—a practice which is on the increase.

Site value: the amount an unencumbered piece of land, less any improvements, is likely to realise at the time of a municipal valuation; the land component of a developed property.

Speculator: a punter who buys property in the expectation of selling it later for a higher price.

Strata title: the title for a segment of a property, a flat, unit or office in which there are several owners. (Nowadays, a separate Torrens title is issued.)

Sub-division: the division of a piece of property into building lots; inevitably this requires several official approvals.

Sub-lease: a property which is already leased is leased again, but not for a longer period than the unexpired part of the original lease.

Survey: the accurate measurement and description of a piece of land, usually showing structures and contours.

Syndicate: a group of investors (individuals or corporations) who get together to invest in a financial project requiring more capital than each one has individually.

Tenancy at will: the tenancy can be closed at will by either landlord or tenant.

Title deeds: the documents proving ownership or property.

Torrens title: named after Sir Robert Torrens of South Australia who put the scheme of registering property titles with governments into effect; it is now used in many parts of the world. Earlier there were General Law or Common Law titles.

Unimproved capital value: the value of a piece of unencumbered land without improvements.

Unregistered mortgage: not registered on the title of the property.

Urban renewal: redevelopment, usually in the more dilapidated sections of cities.

Vendor terms contract: when a property is paid for over time— usually a deposit first, and then regular payments of the balance, plus interest, over several years.

Without prejudice: these words, used during a negotiation, mean that any suggestion or plan put forward cannot be used as evidence later if the negotiations fall down.

Yield: the money you derive by way of income or profit from a property deal.

Zoning: the method by which councils or planning authorities control property use—residential, industrial, etc.

Index